12.95

JUST PLANE CRAZY!

by KIM GOYETTE

Kim Goyette

ISBN: 9798513663416

CONTENTS

This book is dedicated to my incredibly supportive and loving parents, Ellen and Max, who taught me that you can live a very large and meaningful life no matter what your circumstances.

FOREWORD

Travel has always been an important constant in my life. First, as an artist, exhibiting in major art fairs around the globe and second as part of the humanitarian work I do in Cambodia and Nepal. How I wish I knew some of the secrets revealed in this dynamic treasure earlier in my life!

Kim Goyette's decision to share her extraordinary world travel experiences is, without doubt, a gift that requires careful unwrapping! This book is a mindfully constructed manifest of personal growth and adventure and one I could not put down.

Kim and her co-contributor, (hubby Scott), have taken out the mystery, complexity and sometimes hardship from the creation of travel possibilities and have demonstrated how you too can turn your own personal travel dreams into a reality. What I love so much about this couple is their sincerity and playfulness in capturing the essence of travel while weaving in their eclectic and comical personal journey. Kim writes with a tongue-in-cheek sense of humour which makes you fall in love with the Goyette family.

When called to the challenge of stepping out of your own personal comfort zone, Kim provides a warm embrace of safety that is the perfect balance between fear and fearlessness. Through her guidance, the intricacies of world travel seem manageable and attainable.

There is another important aspect to *Just Plane Crazy* which cannot be overlooked... freedom. Kim and Scott make a commitment to create a lifetime experience for their daughter, Kayla, that opens the envelope of limitless possibilities for anyone.

I have always loved the courage of human beings when they play hard and live life to the fullest. Kim digs deeper and opens up a spectrum of life's questions. What do we really value? What is our relevance if we are not happy? How do we want to spend our precious life?

If there is a tiny inkling in your mind of "maybe I want to try?" you will be totally convinced by the end of this book and will definitely want to "GO NOW"!

I have been very blessed to know Scott through his podcast, *The Unfiltered Experience*. And, Kim is a soulful, highly evolved, creative with a heightened sense of being who I admire and feel honored to call a friend.

Patricia Karen Gagic, DStG, is an International Contemporary Artist, Author of *Karmic Alibi*, Chief Visionary Officer of *Help Heal Humanity* and creator of *The Karmic Art Experience*.

INTRODUCTION

"Don't ask what the world needs. Ask what makes you come alive and go do it. Because what the world needs is more people who have come alive." – Howard Thurman

---

My dad slipped a twenty-dollar bill into my hand as he kissed me goodbye.

"Thanks daddy, but I don't really need it," was my response to his generous offer. He and my mom would often try to give me a little extra cash when visiting me at college to help support their "starving" student.

"Take it because I may not have it tomorrow," he would always reply with a big smile.

My younger brother, Gregg, and I grew up in the belief that you might as well enjoy yourself today because you never know what tomorrow will bring. This lighthearted concept inspired many beautiful childhood memories of the four of us hopping into our brown station wagon to go for a Sunday drive with absolutely no destination in mind, always stumbling upon a fun farmer's market or a roadside carnival, where we would make an impromptu pit-stop to experience the festivities.

Some of my favorite family vacations were when my parents would scrounge up a few dollars and we would take a drive up to the Catskill Mountains or down to the Poconos to stay at a cheesy truck-stop motel for the weekend. We would have so much fun in those tacky tourist towns, filling our bellies with junky carnival food like cotton candy and fried dough and participating in corny activities like going to a haunted house or driving bumper boats. We didn't need a lot of money to entertain ourselves. We discovered our most treasured family moments sharing in these spontaneous silly experiences.

Since meeting my husband, Scott, and creating a family of my own, I find that my parents' whimsical view on life has been deeply engrained into my own visions about living.

Life is meant to be enjoyed today.

There is no way to predict what tomorrow will bring. Therefore, it is imperative that we create the deep and meaningful life we desire *now*.

If you have picked up this book, it means you have a spark of interest in living an extraordinary life. You are curious about existing outside the proverbial box and you are ready to take the first step towards living your dreams.

My intention for this book is to inspire people to live beyond their own self-created limits and to venture outside the boundaries of the norm, because in that space magic exists. How do I know this? I know this because I experienced magic first-hand when my family of three took off for one year to travel around the globe.

Through our own personal journey, I have developed this guide to walk you, step-by-step, along the path of manifesting your dream of world travel. Why? It's simple. I want to share the magic.

This guide is your ticket to living your own magnificent story. Don't fear. I will hold your hand throughout the whole process as we maneuver through the stages of world travel manifestation such as *Funding Your Adventure, Picking Your Route, Planning Your Trip, Knowing What to Pack, Choosing the Right Time to Go, Finding Incredible Travel Deals, Homeschooling While on the Road* and more.

Even better, you will learn from all the many hilarious mistakes we made along the way so you can develop plenty of confidence in your own world travel capabilities. If we can do it, you can do it too!

It doesn't matter what life situation you are in, world travel is for **EVERYBODY**. Your financial state, relationship status, job position and family stage have no bearing on your ability to travel the globe in style. All you need is to ignite your imagination and make your dream a reality.

So, let's dive in and see what this world travel thing is all about.

Ready, set, jump!

The Goyette Family!

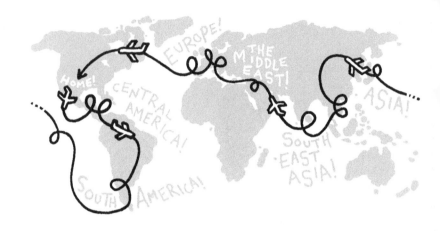

THE LAUNCH OF THE FLYING SQUIRREL
THE BEGINNING

"Jobs fill your pockets, but adventure fills your soul." –
Jaime Lyn Beatty

I returned to the office sopping wet with my co-workers crowding around waiting to hear about our latest wild lunchtime adventure. It all started in the summer of 1995 in Boston, where I met my extremely hilarious husband, Scott. We had only been dating a couple of months and found out quickly that we were both extremely frustrated being stuck in mundane jobs that we attained right out of college. To break the monotony, Scott used to pick me up for lunch at my office every day and we would go do something crazy like jump into a hotel pool with all our work clothes on.

While the summer rolled on our restlessness increased, and our cubicles seemed to grow smaller and smaller by the minute. We felt trapped in the 8am–5pm grind and longed for excitement and freedom, although we had no idea which direction to take.

Three months after our first date, we were perusing through a *Penny Saver* (think of a printed version of Craigslist) and spotted an old RV for sale. Our eyes lit up with the hope of exploration in our future. We had saved $2,600 between the two of us in the short time we had been working, but it was not even close to the $5,000 asking price.

We decided to give it a try anyway, as our life-long motto is "You won't get anything unless you ask." After a conversation with the owner, we found out they were in a bind, moving to Australia in a few days and needed to sell ASAP. We sealed the deal at $2,600 and drove off in a red-striped 1978 Dodge Tioga RV. Its groovy interior decor with retro brown shag rug prompted us to christen our new wheels "The Flying Squirrel". Score!

Scott and I quit our jobs a week later, said goodbye to our families and took off from New York in the beginning of autumn with absolutely no destination in mind. Everyone thought we were crazy. Nonetheless, somehow in their hearts, they believed we would be just fine.

As we made our way down the East Coast to Florida, we had such a blast exploring little towns and meeting interesting people. Without a penny to our names, we had to get creative in discovering the best deals of where to eat and the cheapest places to stay. We often found ourselves playing shuffleboard with retirees, listening to "back in the day" stories while sipping on ice-cold Schlitz beers at random RV parks.

Every place was fresh and exciting to us. Each mile brought new faces, unique food and exceptional fun. The ordinary quickly became the extraordinary and we wanted more.

After four weeks in the Southeast, we hooked a big right on Interstate Highway 10 and headed west towards California. Duct tape became our best friend; we wrapped the silver savior around many parts of our beloved road warrior in lieu of paying costly repairs. On our way, we broke down in a small college town just outside Austin, Texas. On a whim, we decided to stay and go to graduate school.

That trip was the start of more than two decades of endless pee-your-pants belly laughs, practical jokes, emotional meltdowns, explosive farts, eating frenzies, poop talk, animal adventures, insane party nights and a unique plethora of careers. We stayed in Austin and created a beautiful world with our witty daughter, Kayla, and a large recruitment of family members from the East Coast. Until one day we decided to step it up a notch.

A SIX-YEAR DREAM IN THE MAKING
THE INSPIRATION

"The cave you fear to enter holds the treasure you seek." –
Joseph Campbell

Tied down by a mortgage, two car payments and a Kindergartener living under our roof, Scott and I decided to escape our responsibilities for a moment and take a trip to Peru to celebrate my 40th birthday. Connected deeply to nature and fascinated by Incan culture, it had always been my dream to hike Machu Picchu and place my feet on the same trail as the ancient Inca people. The challenge of completing this 14,000-foot elevation trek had definitely been on my bucket list long before I reached my personal four-decade mile-marker.

Several months prior to our journey, I began to train for the physically demanding experience. Yet, I was baffled; where in Austin, Texas can you simulate such rough conditions, high elevations and steep terrain? Absolutely nowhere! With hardly a hill to be found much higher than 425 feet above sea level, this beautiful city could not offer the severe environment I required.

So, I headed to the local middle school and became the crazy lady sprinting up and down the long flight of stairs leading up to the gym. Swarmed by pre-teens, I dodged students making their way to class as I lugged a 30-pound pack up and down my virtual mountain Monday through Friday for three months leading up to our trip.

We had booked a group tour that included a 4-night, 5-day hike along the "Inca Trail" to our final destination, Machu Picchu. We were so excited to leave the daily grind behind for a few days and connect with our adventurous nature once again. On the first day of our escapade, Scott and I congregated at the base of the path to get acquainted with our guides and the participants who would be our teammates for the next several days.

There were people from all over the world; each one with a different reason why they were inspired to take this challenging trek. Hiking in such demanding conditions in such high altitude, rocky terrain and constantly changing weather required us to slow down and reduce our pace, which provided the perfect opportunity to get to know each other. Each person had a story of why this trip was so important to them.

One of my fellow trekkers, Jim, said that he and his dad were supposed to go on the adventure together a few years ago. However, his dad got sick before the trip took place and passed away shortly after. Jim felt compelled to complete the voyage in honor of his father.

An older gentleman, Mike, recently retired, expressed to me that he had wasted his younger years working long hours and not enjoying life enough. He spent all his minutes saving up so that he and his wife could enjoy their golden years together but, not long after he finished his career, his wife passed away and there went his dreams of traveling with her.

Mike regretted not spending more quality time with his partner and his kids. He felt like he had missed out on enjoying the journey of his life, always worrying about the destination. Mike promised himself he would accomplish his lifelong dream of completing the Inca Trail before turning 67 (the maximum age limit for hiking the Trail).

Next, there was Cheryl, a mom of two cute little girls, Jesse in middle school and Sophia in elementary. The three of them were in the middle of a year-long adventure around the world. Cheryl wanted to provide her daughters with an opportunity to experience different cultures and expand their undeveloped perspective of this planet. Each of them had the opportunity to choose a few destinations and one of the girls had selected Machu Picchu.

I was blown away by their bravery. Here they were, three young ladies traveling on their own in foreign lands, with zero access to communication and no one from home knowing where they were. They had left behind everything familiar to them— their friends, family, work, school and home—to go on this incredible escapade of a lifetime. I was mesmerized by their creative courage to go beyond the confines of the conventional Western lifestyle and dare to live large. Larger than large. Extraordinary!

Luckily, I had four days to pick Cheryl's brain about the How's, Who's and What's of this kind of travel. *What are the girls doing for school? How do you have an income while on the road? Who is maintaining your home while you're away? How do you choose where you want to go? What requirements do your daughters need to reenter your school system?*

I felt bad for bombarding Cheryl with my endless questions, but something had sparked a fire inside me. With every step I took on the footpath towards Machu Picchu, I found myself daydreaming about my own family taking our own thrilling journey around the world.

Infinite questions swirled around in my brain. *What age would be the perfect year for Kayla to leave? How could we make this vision work financially? What would we do with our dog and our home? How would we tell our family?*

Catching up with Scott on the trail, I shared my excitement over this fantasy. Not surprisingly, I found out he was imagining the same scenario. We shared our thoughts a little more and both agreed that at some point in the future, our family of three would be taking a year-long expedition of great proportions.

And there the seed of inspiration was planted.

It doesn't matter how you derive your motivation for world travel. What matters is that there is a spark inside you begging to be stoked. If you don't answer the calling now, you run the risk of being sucked into the endless abyss of life's mundane excuses: the "I Can't Syndrome".

I can't because I don't have enough money. I can't because I don't have enough vacation. I can't because I have kids. I can't because I'm not married.

I can't because I am married. I can't because my family will freak. I can't because I have a mortgage. I can't, I can't, I can't!

The bottom line is you can't because you are scared! You're absolutely horrified—and that's a good thing. Good thing you say? How can that be? Well, vast research tells us that our reptilian brain kicks into high gear when presented with an unknown situation. In caveman days, that meant our flight-or-fight mode would switch on when approaching a dark cave or other dubious location in preparation for protecting ourselves from a potential predator.

No wonder why we immediately defend the reasons why we can't go into that dark cave. Or, under these circumstances, why we can't take a year off to travel around the world. Our default form of thinking, one of avoidance, switches on for our own pure protection.

Nowadays we rarely encounter a circumstance where we need to use our reptilian brain for life-or-death situations. The modern application looks a little more like this: You're supposed to go on a first date with someone you met on the Tinder dating app. As you walk into the restaurant, you see a person that resembles their profile picture but only 20-years older. Yikes! The hair on the back of your neck stands up as your creeper radar goes off. Flight mode revs up and you slowly inch your way back to the door, making your grand exodus without being seen. Aaah… the perils of present-day courting.

So, you see, those little Neanderthal naysayers sitting on your shoulder whispering "No" into your ear don't play a major role in your survival rate any longer. Therefore, you don't need to take them so seriously.

3

AN OLD MAN'S TALE

WHEN IS THE RIGHT TIME?

"You can't be that kid standing at the top of the waterslide, overthinking it. You have to go down the chute." – Tina Fey

---

As a requirement to complete my Exercise Science degree at graduate school, I had to take a random education class. It was pretty boring, and I used the time to catch up on sleep throughout the majority of the semester, my eyelids struggling to stay open behind my sunglasses.

One day I walked into the room to find a substitute teacher. His name was Dr. Harris, and I could tell by his silver hair and his stance, hunched over his cane, that he was getting on in years. Dr. Harris was 85 years old and had retired ten-years earlier after a 50-year tenured teaching position. Unable to withstand being away from higher education, he offered to sub on occasion.

Because he had been a professor of education, he was well-versed in the psychology of leading an effective classroom and could easily have taught us about our current topic: "Controlling the Classroom Environment." Instead, he stood in front of our group, his hand shaking as he steadied himself on his cane and fascinated us with a personal story about him and his family.

"I was newly married to the love of my life at the ripe old age of 20, and was an absolute go-getter," he explained. "I wanted to make certain I could care for this beautiful woman and have the means to raise a family of my own. So, I ventured towards a stable career path in education. With our first child born and my undergraduate degree complete, I immediately began a route towards a Masters, hoping someday I could get a position as a professor at a university."

"While attending classes in the evening, I held down two jobs to make ends meet," he continued. "It was such a busy time in my life with very few moments left in the day to spend with my wife and eldest son. Two years passed quickly and at the end, I had earned my desired master's degree with our family expecting another baby on the way."

"Of course, my driven personality wouldn't let me stop there," he resumed. "My final efforts gained me a doctorate and a dream job as a tenure-tracked professor at a university. I took a momentary sigh of relief, knowing I could support my steadily growing family of up to five now."

"As my children sprouted up, I spent the majority of my day with my head down in research and grant applications. While my wife took the three kids to baseball practice and dance recitals, I exhausted most of my weekends at the university library. My beloved begged me to take a break and enjoy some time with our family. But I wanted to increase our savings and guarantee we had enough money for retirement. 'We'll have plenty of quality moments next weekend,' I would always answer."

"By the time the kids were grown and had moved out of the house, I was still full steam ahead on my career goals. My wife pleaded for us to take a vacation. 'We'll go when we retire,' I would consistently reply."

"Fifty years into my career, I finally felt confident about our financial situation and, although I adored teaching, at last I retired. My wife held me to my promise and immediately booked a two-week cruise to explore some tropical islands. Within a month of my retirement and a few days before we were ready to leave on our trip, shockingly, my bride was diagnosed with Alzheimer's," he whispered.

Dr. Harris paused for a moment and you could hear a pin drop in the classroom. We all held our breath, knowing that the outcome would not be good.

"I spent the next five years in and out of doctor's offices as her health rapidly declined. We were confined to our home because she did best in familiar surroundings. I took care of her until my own health prevented me from giving her the proper attention she needed. I spent the final six months of our almost 60-year marriage by her side in a nursing home. She passed peacefully and my heart was crushed."

I could hardly breathe as Dr. Harris finished his story. Tears poured down my face and I looked around at the similarly salt-stained faces of my classmates.

"My point in telling you this," he continued, "is not to upset you, but to wake you up. Time is so short and breezes by you in an instant. Before you know it, years and opportunities slip away if you let them. Don't miss the chance to spend time with the ones you love. Have grand experiences and make incredible memories. Take advantage of your years and *do now*. Don't wait for some unknown safety net in some distant future time. DO NOW!" he exclaimed in a powerful voice.

The bell rang and we all sat still. The words "do now!" echoed in my mind. With a heavy heart, I got up to leave, giving Dr. Harris a sympathetic smile as I passed him. He had no idea how the impact of his words would affect my entire future. His powerful story still echoes through every part of my life.

The only perfect time to accept the grand adventure that awaits you is NOW. There will always be a long list of reasons why some future time is better. But I can assure you that time slips away so fast and next thing you know, 20 years of excuses have passed you by.

Perhaps you are not ready to throw your clothes in a bag, run out and close the door on your familiar life at this very second. World travel does take a teensy-weensy bit of thought and preparation. Yet, the important thing is that you make a plan. Step-by-step you will inch your way towards your intention, the launch date for your extraordinary adventure.

Scott and I knew we wanted to expose Kayla to different cultures, religions, socioeconomic situations and natural experiences so she could develop into an open-minded adult. In addition, she would need to be old enough at the time of our travels to be able to remember her world trip experience. We also wanted her to be more self-sufficient and have enough stamina to make it through the journey. We were aiming to catch her at an age where she was young enough to still enjoy traveling with us, and yet old enough to appreciate everything she was going to absorb.

Also, let's face it, who wouldn't mind missing a year of one of the most tortuous times during one's educational career? Therefore, we thought the transition year into middle school (sixth grade) would be the perfect time for our family. In addition, as a sixth grader, the state curriculum would require her to study world history in social studies. What better way to learn this subject than to explore the world? Bonus!

I marked our intended departure date of June 2018 firmly on the calendar and we were propelled into a six-year mission to plan the experience of a lifetime.

Now, it's time for you to contemplate the intentions for your trip: who will be going along for the ride and what the compelling reasons are for your own blast-off date. Don't let financial concerns get in the way of your travel logistics. Where there's a will, there's a way! I will be discussing tons of options on how to fund your dream excursion in the following chapters but think about the following:

- Brainstorm BIG. Visualize as if all your plans have already fallen into place effortlessly. Don't worry about all the details yet. Just let your imagination flow.
- When is your GO date? Write it down, write it down, write it down!
- Next, say this out loud: "I will be leaving for an extraordinary adventure of a lifetime on _" (fill in the date).

Simple as that! You just took the first leap onto a path of extreme growth and boundless encounters. Awesome job! Now, onto the next stage...baby steps.

Key things to consider

- *Will you be traveling solo or with a companion/your family?*
- *Brainstorm the compelling reasons for your departure date.*
- *Write down your world travel launch date on paper to affirm your vision.*

4

GO TELL IT ON THE MOUNTAIN

BREAKING THE NEWS

"A journey of a thousand miles begins with the first step."–
Confucius

S cott and I decided to break the news to my parents first at
dinner one Friday night. In between a big bite of mashed
potatoes and "could someone pass the salt?" we casually
stated: "Hey guys, guess what? When Kayla is in sixth grade, we
are going to take a year off and travel around the world."

And then... an awkward silence.

As you can imagine, it took a few seconds for my mom and
dad to absorb what we had just said. Then, of course, the
natural response kicked in with a surprised, "What do you
mean?"

After a long description about our inspiration for traveling
the world, our intentions for the trip and why we had chosen the
summer after Kayla's last day of elementary school as our target
date, I could read a combination of excitement and horror
written all over their faces.

My dad, who has some adventure running through his veins,
showed enthusiasm and engaged us in questions about places we
wanted to visit and how long we expected to stay in each country. My mom, on the other hand, kept repeating, "Are you sure

you want to go for a whole year? Why a *whole* year?" To be separated from her only daughter and granddaughter for such an extensive stretch of time appeared to be inconceivable in her mind. I knew that this long stint of travel would have a big impact on my family as we lived only a mile apart and saw each other almost every day. We had not gone more than two weeks without getting together since our daughter was born.

I could feel my mom's anticipated pain. Nonetheless, everyone finished the evening with a light-hearted air about them. After all, this supposed voyage was six years away and so much could change in that time. Why worry about something that may never happen?

Next, I proclaimed our zany idea to my best friend, Alisa. Just like when I announced other crazy travel plans to her in the past, she was overwhelmingly supportive with a hint of dread. No surprise there.

First of all, you should know more about our over 45-year friendship. We met when Alisa was four and I was three. She had just moved into a house up the lane and saw me playing on the street. (Not sure why a three-year old was playing by herself on the road, but I digress.) She walked right up to me and asked if I wanted to be best friends. Of course, I agreed to this stranger's request and we have been inseparable ever since.

We knew from that very moment that we were soul sisters. So, it's no wonder that a year abroad seemed like a lifetime to my forever friend. Nevertheless, just like my parents, she bucked up with a cheerful smile, realizing that 2018 was more than half a decade away.

Our siblings were ecstatic for us. My in-laws reacted like any grandparents who might not see their grandchild for a year, showing concern for Kayla's safety and quality of education during our year-long stint.

In the end, our family members put the idea on the back burner with the understanding that the launch date would be several years away.

On the other hand, our daughter Kayla responded to this unsolicited adventure with a whole different attitude. Scott and I had told her about the incredible mom we met at Machu Picchu who was exploring the world with her grade-school daughters.

We gently mentioned how we dreamed of our family doing the same thing and taking off for a year to travel.

Her kindergarten brain fully understood that this vision of ours meant she would be away from her friends, family and home for a long time, and she did not like the sound of it. In a defiant voice she immediately stated she did not want to go. We told her that if she did not want to come with us she could stay with Grammy and Poppy for a year while we were gone. I could see the wheels in her young head processing the thought of being away from us for so long and she quickly changed her mind. "OK, I'll go if I can get a puppy when we get back," she bargained. We agreed and dropped the subject for a while.

Throughout the following years, we would casually mention our plans to friends and acquaintances. We received a huge array of reactions ranging from jubilation and pure support to absolute disgust that we would take our daughter out of school and expose her to the grave dangers of the world. Nonetheless, no matter what the response, we maintained our determination and continued to discuss our travel strategies with everyone.

One of the best ways to seal the deal on truly manifesting your grand adventure is to tell people about your plans. Inform as many people as you can. The more you announce your dreams out loud to the Universe, the more the Universe will escalate them into fruition.

Here's another strategy for making your plans come true. Voicing your intentions to other humans acts as a HUGE motivator for taking the steps needed to meet your goals. Why? Because once you've made your big announcement, you don't want to disappoint all of your fans.

Feeling accountable to our word was a tremendous driver that propelled Scott and I through challenging times when we wanted to give up on what seemed like an intangible dream. So proclaim your news early and often.

Remember, the naysayers are only reflecting their own personal worries onto you. Believe me, you will uncover plenty of your own doubt throughout the planning process; you don't need someone else's distress to influence you. Their fears are NOT your fears. You were brave enough to take the initial steps towards a lifelong dream. You can be courageous enough to deflect any negative vibes that come your way from those worrywarts.

Now, carry on, full steam ahead!

Key things to consider

- *Tell people about your travel plans and departure date to hold yourself accountable.*
- *Other people's fears are NOT your fears.*
- *You are courageous and bold!*

5

YOUR CREATIVE GENIUS AT WORK

FUNDING YOUR BIG PLANS

"Either find a way or make one!" – Hannibal

My father-in-law, Paul, always says: "Getting old ain't for wussies." In a similar way, planning long-term world travel ain't for the faint-of-heart. I have to admit, the six months prior to our departure date was one of the most stressful times of our lives.

Think about all the things you need to accomplish before leaving on a week-long vacation, like stopping the mail, watering the plants, packing your suitcase and so on. Now imagine all those tasks bulked up 50x on steroids and you've got a six-month endless to-do list in order to prepare yourself, and possibly also your family, for temporarily leaving your everyday life.

Now, please, please, please do not let those words discourage you from manifesting your dreams. Yes, the months leading up to "go time" will be challenging as all hell. Still, in the end, I can promise you, your experiences while traveling will be worth any pain and suffering you endure through the developmental period. Therefore, my intention for this chapter is to assist you in making the process as easy as possible by walking you through all the dos and don'ts, so you can avoid the mistakes that we made along the way.

I would say, before we hit the six-month countdown mark, we

had not really put much effort into the planning of our year-long adventure. Of course, we had developed some general ideas about how we would sustain ourselves on the road, listed some countries we wanted to visit and thought about where we would like to start. However, 99.9 percent of our preparation efforts came together in the 180-days approaching blast-off.

That being said, there are several important factors you need to consider before you enter crunch time. Number one on the list is your financial situation: *How will you support yourself while abroad?*

Now, don't fret about your current monetary state. You don't have to be a millionaire to enjoy the luxury of long-term travel. Furthermore, you don't need huge savings stocked away in the bank.

How do I know this? Because the Goyettes are just ordinary people who achieved an extraordinary thing on an average income. We generate common middle-class earnings. Moreover, I can assure you, we did not have a stash of money saved in the bank or a long-lost relative who passed away and left us a chunk of dough.

We stepped away from our typical lives, leapt out of our comfort zone and travelled around the entire globe for one year. During that time, we visited 26 countries, explored 49 cities, slept in 87 different beds and saw things that we never imagined in our wildest dreams could exist on this planet.

If you are enticed at the idea of experiencing exotic food, diverse cultures and majestic landscapes, then you will find a method to fund your adventure. Where there's a will, there's a way. Simple as that!

For us, we had a three-fold revenue generating plan to bring us income while touring. The first two parts were to rent out both of our residential properties, our home and a small cabin in the country that we owned. The second was for me to work part-time while traveling; I planned to continue supporting a client that I partnered with through my sales consulting business.

Austin is a pretty hot market when it comes to real estate and rentals. So, we didn't think we would have any problems finding someone to move into our two properties, but we had a few constraints that soon posed some challenges we hadn't expected.

We knew we were only going to be gone for one year and we didn't want the hassle of moving all our furniture out of our properties for such a short amount of time. So, we elected to rent our homes fully furnished.

Although short-term vacation rentals can be more lucrative, they are also high-risk when it comes to exposing your personal belongings to random guests. We decided that a long-term, full-year rental would be ideal for us and less effort in the long run.

We partnered with Sam, a great property manager, who would be responsible for finding renters and maintaining the properties while we were away. We wanted to have as much freedom while we were vagabonding and had no desire to be bogged down with collecting rent or upkeep issues. We preferred a low-maintenance scenario, where someone else handled every-thing back home, so we could maximize time for exploration and fun.

We put the properties up for lease about four months prior to go-time. Then we waited, and waited, and waited. The months quickly ticked by with very little activity from potential renters. It turned out that a fully furnished home ended up being a hindrance instead of an enhancement because most people looking to move already had their own stuff. In addition, a one-year lease term narrowed the playing field when searching for the perfect living arrangements. Scott and I started to get a little nervous. We were really counting on the rentals to be the major income for our roadshow.

We continued to plug away at the endless list of tasks that we needed to accomplish for our future renters. The upside? Making your home rent-ready was the perfect opportunity for a mini-malist like me to get rid of tons of junk that cluttered our home and had taken up unnecessary space. We purged, we painted and we prepped every inch of our living space to attract the ultimate tenants. Our homes were impeccable. They had never looked so good. There was something about the fear of having no income to fund our grand vision that elevated our motivation to make every millimeter of our properties spic-and-span.

Over the next couple of months, we had a few showings, but there was always some special request that killed the deal, like moving all of our living room furniture out, or allowing the renters' four shedding dogs to be residents too. Although we were desperate to fill the lease, we were very particular about finding someone who would treat our homes like they were their own. Being first-time landlords, we may have set our expectations of returning to Texas after one year with our homes in perfect condition a little too high. But we didn't care. We were willing to wait for someone who would love our homes as much as we did.

That is, until it was only three weeks before we were supposed to hop on a one-way plane ride to Costa Rica and there were no prospective tenants in the mix. Scott and I were panicked. It was truly getting down to the wire. We absolutely had to rent both homes in order to pull off our plans.

One morning, I sat on my back deck and did the only thing I knew that was left to do. I just threw everything out to the Universe.

"We will find the perfect people to move into our homes, who will care for them like they are their own," was my mantra for the next 20 minutes.

Later that day, a fellow professor of Scott's suggested we post the listings on www.sabbatical.com, which is a VRBO-like site limited to higher education faculty who want to take a temporary leave-of-absence from their position. Within an hour of publishing the listing, we received a request to view our main home. An extremely nice couple arrived the next day. He was the president of a university, and they were planning to take off for some time to move closer to their grandchild. As we showed them our home, everything seemed to fall into alignment.

She absolutely loved gardening and offered to care for my prized possessions—my back yard garden and indoor plants—while we were traveling. He matched the lofty height of my husband's basketball physique and liked that all our furniture fit him perfectly. They had one very sweet, non-shedding dog. They needed our residence for one year, from June to June, the exact timeframe we were going to be away. In addition, they were ecstatic that our home was fully furnished as they were planning on using our place part-time and didn't want to fuss with all the fittings.

It was a match made in heaven! *Universe, oh Universe, I bow down to your magnificent power!* The application went through without a hitch and their move-in date was finalized. Just like that, my heart jump-started and began beating again.

I had spoken with my consulting client several months prior

to explain our plans to be on the move for a year. My hope was that they would let me continue working part-time while we were traveling. With some deep explanation and a little coercing, they had graciously agreed to continue the partnership under the understanding that my productivity would not change. What a relief! Two down, one to go! We completed the final details for the rental of our primary home and put our last box of personal items into storage in our garage.

With just one week before we were set to leave, we still had not leased our cabin. Although it would be a bit of a financial struggle to survive with just two out of our three planned income sources, we vowed we would make it happen.

Just 24-hours before leaving on our trip I sat by myself on our deck to soak up the beauty of my backyard garden—the space I call my spiritual temple—one last time. I breathed in the sweet fragrance of the trailing honeysuckle flowers with the understanding that I would not absorb the familiar scents of home for a whole year.

Feelings of anxiety rose within me as the thought of not renting our cabin crept into my mind. With a final effort, I closed my eyes to connect deeply with the abundance of the Universe and tap into my powerful mantra: "We will find the perfect person to move into our cabin who will care for it like it is their own."

Finally, the big day had arrived! We gathered in the living room to take one final look at our home, and then shut our front door and locked it behind us. It was such a weird feeling to literally close the door on our old life and walk away. We had no idea what lay ahead of us. All we knew was that it was guaranteed to be a big adventure.

My parents drove us to the airport, and with heavy hearts and tears in our eyes we said our goodbyes. This would be the longest time we would ever have been separated from each other. We threw our hefty backpacks on our backs, each of us grabbed our carry-on bag and headed through the airport doors. As they closed behind us, our new reality finally sunk in.

We had no permanent address to call our home. Nothing tied us to any single destination. We were totally free to travel the world.

We hopped on the plane; first stop, Costa Rica! As we started to take off, I heard the ding of a text from my phone. I looked down to see a message from our property manager. "We rented the cabin!" he declared.

Oh mighty, mighty Universe! I am so incredibly grateful for all of your tremendous gifts, I thought to myself. I shared the unbelievably good news with Scott. He grabbed my hand and we both broke into huge grins. Resolving our financial trifecta was such a relief. We watched the view of downtown Austin quickly disappear out of sight. All our tension and worry rapidly vanished as we sank comfortably into our seats knowing this would be the grandest ride of our lives.

Now, you may be in a completely different financial situation than we were going into this trip. Maybe you don't have a home to rent. Or, possibly, you don't have a flexible job that allows you to work outside of the office. Do not fret! We met tons of other world adventurers on this beautiful planet who were funding their dreams in every possible way imaginable.

When we were in Greece, we encountered a couple with two little girls who had sold everything back in the Netherlands, bought a decked-out van and were driving across Europe for a year. They both did a little freelance work while traveling though most of their funding came from selling their home and many of their possessions to afford them the freedom of an extended holiday.

Does that sound too extreme for you?

Then let me introduce you to a young entrepreneur from San Francisco who we met in Austria while sharing an Uber ride. He had let go of his expensive apartment lease and set off with a goal to visit all of Eastern Europe within the next six months. He had told his high-tech client that he would be telecommuting from home, and they never knew the difference. He invested the money he saved on rent to explore one of the most affordable regions on the planet. This gave him the ability to live like a king throughout his journey.

Then there was the woman we met on the coast of Colombia. She had released all her monetary ties with her home in Canada, got certified as a masseuse and used those skills to earn a living while wandering from beach town to beach town in Central and South America. She mindfully built her travel plans based on her desire to be free to go anywhere at any time.

Do none of these situations resonate with your current status? I can give you endless examples of characters we chanced upon on our nomadic journey, each with a unique method of subsidizing their lifelong dreams of world travel. Bottom line: where there is a will, there is a way.

When you consider your present career and financial condition as an opportunity, not a burden, the doors of creative thinking will swing wide open. Ruminate on this for a while. If you are living in an apartment, then you could have all the freedom in the world to roam the planet when your lease is up. If you own a home, then you may have a chance for a consistent rental income while you travel.

If you have a career as a healthcare professional such as a nurse, doctor or dentist, choose a country that needs your services, exchange homes with another family from that area through www.homeexchange.com and take off for 6–12 months to work abroad while someone manages your business back home.

If you have a special wellness certification as a yoga or fitness instructor or massage therapist, hop on fitnessprotravel.com and exchange your services for luxury accommodations at high-end resorts in the Caribbean, Mexico, Southeast Asia and Central America. I taught yoga at a fabulous all-inclusive resort in Costa Rica for three weeks during our travels. It was absolutely wonderful and practically free. In exchange for teaching two yoga classes per day, our family (maximum two adults and two children) enjoyed a luxurious vacation for only $600 per week. This package, typically valued at $3,500, included a beautiful room with a view, all scrumptious meals, top shelf drinks and entertainment activities. It is an awesome deal!

If you are an expert in your industry, but are required to be in the office, you could instead take your show on the road by working as a freelance consultant. If you are tied to a desk job where you have to go into work every day, then quit! Go get certified in a passion you love to do and travel to destinations that desire those specialized services. If you have a job where you can work from anywhere in the world, well that answers that question...go for it!

You see, no matter how you slice it, there is an income opportunity for every situation. Moreover, where there is opportunity, there is hope and where there is hope, there is inspiration to get'er done. So, go get'er done!

Key Things to Consider

- *Contemplate how your current living situation could be an opportunity for income.*
- *Ponder a creative twist on your present job that will provide the flexibility to travel.*
- *Consider your passions and hobbies as a potential source of income.*

6

ADVICE FROM A TRAVEL GURU
AN ADVENTURE OF A LIFETIME WITH ZERO DEBT

"Logic will get you from A to B. Imagination will take you everywhere." – Albert Einstein

---

During the one year that the Goyette family vagabonded around the globe, we took 47 flights, slept in 87 different accommodations, engaged in stellar, blow-your-mind experiences and returned to the United States with absolutely **ZERO** debt.

"How is that possible?" you ask.

It's possible because we are the type of family that only spends money we actually possess.

"Well, then you must have been staying in low-end hostels and found cheap airline tickets smooshed in the back of the plane near the toilet," you say.

My response to that is, "First-class baby, (almost) all the way!"

We lived like royalty while we were traveling. In most cases, we had a much better quality of life than back in the States. We stayed in deluxe hotels at beachfront properties and the classiest Airbnbs in downtown cities. We had the luxury of flying business or first class for the majority of our flights. We dined on the finest cuisine and indulged in gourmet food from every culture. We did once-in-a-lifetime activities like exploring the Pyramids in Egypt, bathing elephants in Thailand, feasting on an epicurean picnic at the base of the Torres del Paine mountains in Patagonia and jaunting off on a helicopter to go blue-whale-watching in Sri Lanka. We would never have been able to afford these incredible experiences abroad if we were living at home in the United States.

Moreover, we did it all on a budget of $60 per day for food and $60 per day for accommodations. Unbelievable, right? Our daily travel budget was so much cheaper than our daily living expenditures back in Austin.

How did we do it? Let me introduce you to my personal travel agent and lifelong partner in adventure: my husband, Scott.

Scott and I have been together for more than 25 years. In that time, he has developed a magnificent and highly valuable superpower: the ability to find incredible travel deals. From his expertise in choosing the right credit cards that earn us free accommodations, airport lounge access and first-class airline tickets, to getting the most bang for our buck when it comes to using our airline points, he is a master at his craft.

For example, he found a last-minute, first class airline ticket on Turkish Airlines for free using points. It included a full-day tour of Istanbul with a Turkish breakfast and lunch, and entrance to the absolute best airport lounge I have ever experienced where we were lavished with an extensive buffet of gourmet Turkish cuisine, as well as massages, entertainment and more. The experience was so wonderful. We were hoping our flight would be delayed so we could enjoy the fabulous amenities longer.

I attest 100 percent of our luxury travel experience to Scott's unparalleled gift of discovering extravagant experiences at discount prices. Therefore, I thought it would be best to hand this chapter over to my deal-sniffing hound, so you can get this important information straight from a professional. Take it away Scott!

Thanks so much for the intro, Kim.

My wife of more than two decades fully understands that I am all about sports. Whether it's playing basketball with my friends or tossing a football on the beach, I am truly in my element when playing games. And that is exactly what affordable travel is all about. It's nothing more than playing a game.

While there are no actual rules to the game, there are definitely many methods to find truly extraordinary travel experiences. Simply put, it all begins with your willingness to dive deeper into your destination and accommodation searches and discover an abundance of hidden vacation gems – all over the planet. And just like any other game, being a travel detective is always more enjoyable when you make it fun. So, let's have some fun and play the GAME!

Gain Alliances
Acquire Points
Monitor Your Spending
Explore Alternatives

Gain Alliances

About a year prior to our global departure, I began doing a lot of research, focused on which credit cards, airlines, hotels and rental-car companies offered the best loyalty programs with the most perks. Then, I registered for these top programs and started earning points on every dollar spent and each vacation taken. It was surprising how quickly points accumulated once we put all our spending eggs in one common basket.

We rolled all of our monthly expenditures—like utilities, groceries, gas and other big-ticket purchases—onto one airline-specific credit card and one hotel-specific credit card to help us earn enough points to start our year-long adventure with three free international business-class flights and enough extra points for a few short haul flights later in our journey, as well as more than 20 free nights for hotel stays. Throughout our travels, we continued to build on those rewards by accumulating more points for all our flights, hotel stays and credit card expenditures while on the road. This is how you can gain wealth by establishing mindfully selected alliances.

Credit Cards

Choose credit cards that offer the most points for purchases and offer the greatest travel benefits such as point bonuses, cheaper redemption options for reward travel, airport lounge access, hotel upgrades, automatic elite status with partner airlines and the ability to earn higher-level elite status through dollars spent. At the time of our travels, we selected the United Presidential Plus and Marriott Bonvoy credit cards to accelerate our point earnings. You will have to do your own research to see which card is best for you at the time of your travels, as offers change daily. There is always at least one exceptional offer out there. Just take the time to do the research.

Airlines

Investigate the routes to where you want to go and then establish an alliance with the airlines that have the best flights to those destinations. Align yourself with their loyalty program and start earning points every time you fly. When you build status with an airline you may receive upgrades for yourself and one or more companions, depending on the program and status level. These upgrades can be for seats with more room, closer to the front of the plane, and/or in first class.

Another perk is that you will be allowed as many as three checked bags for free. Some status levels will offer airport lounge access as well, especially if sitting in a premium seat. This is a huge benefit when you have a long layover and need to crash. There are also credit cards that enable free lounge access, which ours did. In addition, you will earn points for free flights and the higher the status, the better the chance of getting the flights of your choice. So, all in all, the more you fly, the more you receive.

At the time of our travels, the One World Alliance (American Airlines and partners) had tons of flights to and within South and Central America, while the Sky Team Alliance (Delta and partners) had more affordable routes to Europe. The Star Alliance (United and partners), on the other hand, had great prices and routes to Asia and Southeast Asia and had the biggest worldwide alliance program overall. This is an example of popular routes with the three major domestic airlines and their alliances, but we also found some of our best flight deals on promotional offers with international airlines, such as Turkish Airlines, Emirates, Thai Airways, SriLankan Airlines and Singapore Airlines.

Hotels

While there are a lot of independent and smaller boutique hotels, the three largest players in the hotel game that offer the most benefits are the Hilton Family of Hotels, Bonvoy (which was formed by the Marriott and SPG merger) and the Hyatt Family of Hotels. Developing an alliance with these hotel groups will get you accommodations in almost any city in the world. We chose Marriott and Hilton as our go-to hotel brands. In addition to multiple hotel stays prior to our year-long journey, we chose a Marriott-branded credit card and were able to achieve Platinum status through them and Diamond status with Hilton (mostly due to hotel stays and bonus points from promotions). These status levels earned us suite upgrades, free breakfasts, and amazing happy hours and light dinners with every stay throughout our trip around the world.

Rental Cars

Just like other alliances, choosing one or two rental car companies will earn you amazing upgrades, better rates and free rentals, but not all international brands like Hertz, Avis, Alamo and Budget offer the same benefits in all countries. We received amazing benefits in Europe and other touristy destinations, but our alliance was not honored in countries like Costa Rica (since they literally license the name but do not offer the same service).

Acquire Points

Right now, airlines, hotels and credit card alliances are offering insane point bonuses towards free-night stays and instant elite status when certain thresholds are met. Continued loyalty can help you stack up points and benefits with airlines and their partners. One example is the United Presidential Plus credit card, which allowed us to earn Elite status on United with money spent plus miles flown, and gives us Gold status instantly with Marriott Bonvoy and President's Circle with Hertz, which is the highest status they offer. Not to mention, we have access to United lounges nationwide and Star Alliance clubs worldwide.

So, just imagine, with this one card alone, we could enter the airport and hang out in a premier lounge enjoying free drinks and snacks while we waited for our flight. Onboard, we could experience all the perks of sitting in a first-class seats with extra room, great service and delicious meals. Then we could arrive at our destination and pick up a luxury, upgraded car and finally check into a five-star Marriott hotel and enjoy extravagance at its finest. Selecting the right alliances can gain you perks galore.

Constantly checking with your loyalty program for multipliers or bonuses will help you accumulate more points, so stay on top of it. Taking advantage of these offers is an easy way to get ahead quickly. Although this may seem like a lot of work, once you get your system down, it is no harder than checking your email once per week for updates to program offers and it will help expand your affordable travel efforts exponentially.

Monitor Your Spending

When it comes to the affordable travel GAME, you have to think of your loyalty points as real currency. You might find a free hotel night in downtown Paris for 50,000 points. But, if you do your research, there are plenty of less touristy destinations where you can, for example, stay four nights for 10,000 points per night and get the fifth night free on reward stays. So, in essence you only pay 8,000 per night. This mindful point redemption method gained us almost two free months of Hilton hotel stays in less traveled, but still incredibly beautiful destinations like Krakow and Warsaw in Poland, Sibiu in Romania, and Valencia in Spain.

Uncovering Hidden Gems

Arrange your trip around value-based locations. Explore countries that have a devalued currency and go there. Every place in the world is worth exploring. This open mindset brought us to some of our most unexpected favorite countries on the planet like Cambodia, Sri Lanka and Guatemala. We were initially drawn to these countries because of their amazing travel value and fell in love with the people, culture and cuisine of each. So, find the greatest deals and just go.

Except for visiting Paris, London and Tokyo to honor Kayla's top-three must-see destinations, we often chose less-traveled cities to explore. Instead of visiting more costly metropolitans like Barcelona, we had an enchanting experience in the affordable Spanish city of Valencia and village of Murcia. Both offered incredible scenery, culture and culinary experiences and we would absolutely return to them in the future. Uncovering hidden gems is definitely one way to make your travel dollars stretch for miles.

Never Say Never

Prior to travel, be cautious about listening to advice from others. Many people told us not to visit certain countries due to supposed safety issues. Having done our own research about a given country's level of tourist safety, we often chose to go anyway and had some of the most satisfying experiences of our trip. Based on other peoples' fears, countries like Romania, Colombia, Cambodia and Guatemala were highly discouraged by our friends and family. But, upon arrival, we quickly realized that the news reports about these destinations were over-dramatized and these countries fostered some of the fondest memories of our trip.

From Pauper to Prince

When you establish your daily spending budget for your adventure, it does not mean you need to spend that *exact* amount every day. Leaving a little wiggle room will allow you to save some money one day so you can splurge on another day. For example, we stayed in a cheaper apartment for a week in Santiago so we could enjoy more extravagant accommodations when we were in Patagonia.

Another way to offset your daily cost of living is to get free breakfast and evening Hors d'oeuvres at hotels (due to having elite status). This provides an opportunity to shift your daily spending dollars to save up for special experiences. Remember, if you meet your total monthly budget, it does not matter how you got there, so get creative.

Explore Alternatives

Flexibility is key when it comes to snagging travel bargains. An open mind will take you to places you never thought existed on the planet and expand your travel experience exponentially. Look for the places you never thought you would go and accept diversions to your journey. Those unintentional detours will be the places you talk about forever.

Hotels vs. Airbnbs

Sometimes it's fun to live like the locals and rent an Airbnb. We often found ourselves in a cute little beachfront condo or a quaint house in the country for some of our longer stays. Then we would shift gears and check into a five-star Marriott or Hilton for the weekend so we could regroup and enjoy the amenities. All our booking decisions were based on finding general areas we wanted to visit and then discovering accommodations that made sense for that time in our trip.

First, I focused my attention on what our family wanted most in the moment—like access to a pool, free breakfast, our own kitchen or an exercise and laundry facility. Then, I would zoom in on off-peak or low-cost-living destinations. Finally, I would look at accommodation options located just outside of touristy areas that created better value. This technique allowed our family to stay in first class accommodations at fabulous places like Valparaiso, Chile or Mendoza, Argentina for pennies on the dollar.

Online Booking Agencies

If you do not have enough time before your big trip to build up loyalty points with major hotel brands, alliances with online booking agencies are a great way to go. You can receive rebates, credit towards future stays, free Global Entry (allows easy entry into the United States based on a prior background check) and upgrades for hotels with an easy to earn VIP status. Online booking agencies such as Orbitz, Expedia, Travelocity and Booking.com provide an opportunity for you to search for great deals anywhere in the world and have much lower status thresholds than going direct with a hotel brand (of course, the benefits are not quite as amazing...but it's still worth it).

Flexibility is imperative when finding travel deals, so expand your mind to alternate destinations and follow the bargains. Affordable travel is a by-product of finding the path least traveled. Similarly, cost-effective travel is often to be had by looking where others are not for great deals. An example of this, as I mentioned earlier, is not being afraid to organize your trips around value destinations versus choosing destinations and then trying to create value. Just for fun, do a search on one of the online booking agencies for top travel deals in the world and see what comes up. Find an enticing deal and start your travel plans there.

From choosing the best credit card to finding excellent point-redemption value, digging deeper will win you the travel deals you desire. For example, initially our family wanted to fly from Dubai to Tel Aviv to visit Kim's cousin. I almost spent 35,000 points per person for economy seats, but I kept looking. It turned out that United's Star Alliance Partner, Turkish Airlines, had a deal for first-class tickets for only 30,000 points per person, which included access to a premier airport lounge and a tour of Istanbul. On the way we had a 24-hour layover in Cairo and even took a tour of the Pyramids. I found this bargain first-class experience because I was willing to be flexible and detour from my original route. I suggest shifting your mindset to go where the deals are and you will create a journey filled with adventure and wonder.

I could easily tell you exactly which hotels we booked, which flights we took and the specifics of how I made sure our family sat in first-class seats, stayed in the best hotels and truly lived the dream. I could let you in on every move I made, but deals change daily, so understanding the mindset of the GAME will take you much further in satisfying your thirst for affordable travel. Now, go get'em!

~

Key Things to Consider

- *Choose one or two credit cards that have the most perks with their loyalty program and roll all your expenditures onto those cards to start earning points.*
- *Select alliances with airlines, hotels and rental car companies that offer the most benefits in your selected destinations.*
- *Think of your points as real currency and spend them mindfully to enhance your opportunity for affordable and free travel.*
- *Search for less touristy destinations to visit during off-peak season for additional savings.*

7

A MINIMALIST'S DREAM

WHAT TO PACK

"He who travels happily must travel light." – Antoine de
Saint Exupery

One of the biggest challenges of our travel preparations
was packing our whole life into a single carry-on and
one backpack per person. I thought I was pretty good
about selecting only the bare essentials to put in my luggage – I
chose a space in our guest room and over several months prior to
our departure date I added items to the must-have pile. I also
bought some packing cubes, which help keep your garments
organized in your baggage. I began to fill them with the clothes I
was bringing, and my limited wardrobe fit perfectly into each
square.

Just a few days before our departure, our friends, Greg and
Michelle, came over with their kids to say goodbye. I had the
filled packing squares sitting next to my baggage. Greg asked if I
had tried to fit them into the carry-on yet and began stuffing
them into the tiny bag. I was shocked to see that he could barely
fit one out of the five squares in there. Crap! Now I had to
rethink the whole packing thing.

I stayed up all night pulling "essentials" out of the bag and
putting them in the newly created "do not absolutely need" pile.
I whittled it all down to a handful of socks and underwear, a pair

each of flip flops and sneakers, a couple of pairs of pants and long-sleeve shirts, one micro-down lightweight jacket, a few sets of yoga clothes, three bathing suits, a computer, a first aid kit, a small toiletry bag and my phone. Gone were the exercise bands, water filter, books, foam roller, travel hammock, picnic blanket in a bag, my good camera and other do-dads I thought were necessary items for a year's worth of travel.

My daughter Kayla had no problem fitting her tiny clothes and shoes in her bag. She even had room for her slime collection, tons of games and art supplies for the year. Scott, on the other hand, with his size 14 shoes and XXL clothes, was only able to take a miniscule amount. Nevertheless, I was proud of all of us for slimming things down and making it work. Wow! What a weird and liberating feeling it was to be able to carry everything we needed for a year in our hands. This packing process taught me two big lessons.

First, that you need very few "things" to live a full and satisfying life. Collecting stuff provides only temporary happiness. It's the quality of the people you surround yourself with and the experiences you engage in that truly create a meaningful life story.

Second, the less you have, the less you have to worry about. Leaving behind the few valuables we owned provided us with a huge sense of freedom from anxiety that typically comes with worry over losing your stuff. In addition, gone was the stress that goes with managing and maintaining that stuff.

I have compiled a list to help ease your packing process:

Light is Right – Luggage

In order for you to select the correct luggage for your needs, think about what type of travel you will be doing. Will you be constantly on the move or staying put in the same place for a long period of time? If you plan to hop around a lot, I highly suggest you consider the smallest, lightest luggage possible.

Originally, we thought we would each have a backpack and then one large suitcase. However, we quickly dismissed that idea after realizing we would have to check the big bag in every time we flew. Instead, we each chose one small rolling carry-on bag by Travelpro and a durable backpack by High Sierra. We wanted to avoid being held up at airports due to lost or delayed checked luggage. In addition, our focus was to reduce the risk of someone stealing our belongings, since we needed them for the whole year.

Minimalism at Its Finest – Less is More

Each of us was responsible for carrying our own luggage for the entire trip, which made us think hard about packing extra items that were not absolutely necessary. Remember, every pound you pack is an extra pound you have to carry. When it comes to backpack weight, less is absolutely more for surviving the added heaviness on your shoulders.

On travel days, wear your bulkiest clothes and shoes, so you can fit more stuff into your luggage. We could often be seen loaded up with three layers of clothes, jackets and sneakers on steamy hot days as we boarded airplanes.

Back Off the Bling – Valuables

Leave ALL valuables behind. This includes flashy jewelry, expensive cameras and desirable but unnecessary technology. I locked up my wedding ring in a safe back home and chose one pair of inexpensive earrings, one stone necklace and one beaded bracelet to wear for the year. We left our good Nikon camera at home for two reasons: it took up too much space and it would draw the attention of potential thieves.

Slim It Down – Purses and Wallets

Along with personal valuables, while traveling you want to be very discreet about your purse and/or wallet. I chose a very small, cross-chest purse from Bagallini, about the size of a large wallet. It provided plenty of zippered compartments that could hold my passport, phone, cash and credit cards and that's it. I loved that I could easily hide it under my clothes if need be, and it would be harder for someone to steal while I was wearing it in the front of my body.

We had heard that you should always carry two wallets, one with just a little bit of cash in it so you can hand it over if you're robbed. However, Scott just brought his regular wallet, and we never had a problem with theft the entire time we traveled. I credit our luck to keeping a low profile and being aware of our surroundings at all times.

I Have a Boo Boo – First Aid Kit

Make a first aid kit with the bare basics that include a thermometer, bandages, antibacterial cream, anti-itch cream, tweezers, antihistamine, ibuprofen and acetaminophen. Add any special remedies to address specific allergic reactions. You will find things like bandages all over the world, so don't worry about filling your bag with that kind of stuff.

Anyone Got My Scripts – Medications and Supplements

Most insurance companies will not let you get more than a three-month supply of prescription medications at one time. Talk to your doctor and medical insurance provider well before you are ready to leave to let them know of your plans and see if they can make an exception. It is hard to fill U.S.-based prescriptions internationally. That being said, in many countries it is very easy to make an appointment with a local doctor and get a script filled at a neighborhood pharmacy. Still, keep in mind that they may not have access to the prescription you need.

In addition, it is very challenging to get a wide range of supplements overseas. Scott and I thought we would be able to find simple vitamins like B-Complex and Vitamin D + K, but we had a hard time tracking them down. Pack your essentials—your must-have medication and vitamins— on the basis that you may not gain access to a pharmacy or store for the duration of your trip.

Check, Check and Recheck – Documentation

Make certain your passport does not expire within six months of the end of your trip. This is VERY important. We did not realize that many countries will prevent you from entering if your passport expires in less than six months. You can find a very stressful story about this personal blunder under the chapter "Mistakes to Avoid Along the Way".

In addition, bring extra passport photos for every person traveling. This is useful, just in case you lose your documentation and will save you a lot of time searching for a photo shop. Some countries require you to provide a passport-size picture to gain an entry visa.

Vroom Vroom – Driver's License

Make sure at least one person in your traveling party has a valid driver's license. You will not be able to rent a vehicle if you do not have one handy. Again, make certain it is not due to expire within the timeframe that you will be traveling by car. We made that mistake while abroad and had to rush-order one for Scott from the States.

Lighten Your Load – Day Bags

Take one small day bag, like a tote bag or reusable shopping bag. It's nice to leave your large backpack behind at the hotel and just take the essentials when you are exploring a new city. In addition, many countries require that you provide your own bag when shopping.

Shine a Little Light on the Situation – Flashlight

You never know where you are going to end up on your adventure. Having a flashlight on hand could prevent you from getting lost in the jungle or assist your safe descent down a mountain at night.

Avoid the Jolt – Adapters

Most countries outside the U.S. use 220 voltage instead of 120 voltage. That means if you try to plug into a high voltage outlet using a low voltage plug, you most likely will see a lot of smoke and possibly catch your electronics on fire. That concern is easily resolved by using an electrical adapter.

The challenge is that, although many countries use 220 voltage, their outlet shapes are totally different from one another. Some have three prongs strait in a row; some have three fat prongs in a triangle. It's important to know the typical electrical outlet for a country before you visit, so you can buy the right adapter. It's surprising, but in many remote areas there are no adapters to be found. We got stuck searching for days in Chile until we located one.

Instead of lugging around a different adapter for each country, I highly recommend buying a Universal Travel Adapter that can be used in 99 percent of the places you visit. Having a couple of these babies will save you significant time and money, while venturing. I suggest having at least one for each person.

I've Got the Power – Chargers

You can bring all the gadgets that you want but if you do not have the appropriate charger, your electronics will be of no use. Pack all your chargers and backups too. Be warned, in foreign lands there is not an iPhone store on every corner therefore, it is challenging to find replacement chargers while abroad. Also, add an HDMI cable to your packing list. We used one at several Airbnbs to stream Netflix from our computer onto a flat-screen TV.

The Fun has Just Begun – Games and Entertainment

There will be plenty of downtime during long train rides, international flights, extensive delays at the airport or restaurants, and rainy days at hotels. You'll want something to pass the time, especially if you are traveling with kids. We brought a handful of small games that were versatile and could be played in several different ways like a deck of cards, five dice, Jenga blocks, Uno and Spot It. To conserve packing space, you can also download game apps to your smart device like Millionaire and Headsup. If you are traveling with kids, art supplies are also a must. We got a lot of use out of colored pencils, watercolor paint and markers.

Do not bother lugging around actual books; it's just extra weight in your suitcase. I would definitely recommend downloading Kindle or other similar reading apps on your phone so you will have all of the books and audiobooks you want at your fingertips. One book that I did bring was a diary to journal about all our adventures. Alternatively, you could easily do this on your computer. Personally, I prefer having a physical log of our memories.

This list is just some of the basics you will need during your long-term travel. Before you pack, think about what you and your travel companions use on a daily basis. Then, do some research to see if these products are easily accessible internationally. Consider the range of climates and terrain you will encounter. A little contemplation during your pre-trip preparations will give you the guidance you need to choose your packing items wisely.

Key Things to Consider

- *To determine if you truly need to pack an item, ask yourself: "Am I willing to carry this with me for my entire journey?"*
- *Leave all valuables at home.*
- *Make certain all your documentation is valid.*
- *Bring plenty of backup chargers and outlet adapters.*

8

THE LIST WE FINALLY WHIPPED

IMPERATIVE THINGS TO DO BEFORE YOU LEAVE

"When eating an elephant, take one bite at a time." –
Creighton Abrams

As I sit here writing this chapter, I am laughing at the title because when you are planning a year-long trip around the world, *everything* seems imperative. I spent tons of hours and energy developing and checking off an infinite list of tasks that needed to be accomplished before go-time.

In an effort to save you some time in the research department, I thought I would share a catalog of items that should be completed before you depart on your grand escapade. Here we go…

To Inject or Not to Inject – Vaccines

There is a huge worldwide debate on whether vaccinating is the right thing to do. No matter where you are on the spectrum, you will need to think about where you are traveling and if location-specific immunizations will be needed. Do your research on the countries you will be visiting as some require you to have specific vaccinations to be able to enter. Many countries put restrictions on visitors trying to cross over their borders if they are traveling from another country that has a high infection rate of a transmittable disease. This was the case when I researched Thailand's yellow fever vaccination requirements if arriving from a high-risk region, so we had to plan the sequence of our travels accordingly and choose our route wisely.

That being said, I spent a good amount of time looking at immunization requirements and risks for each country we wanted to explore. Personally, I do not like to over-vaccinate, so trying to choose the correct immunizations that would reduce my family's potential exposure to ailments was stressful for me. Based on my risk analysis, we chose to vaccinate for food/water-borne diseases such as hepatitis A and typhoid. Ultimately, you will have to select the correct vaccination regime that meets your comfort level.

Hey, I'm On Vacation – Travel Alerts

Make sure to contact the customer service department of each credit card you plan to use while traveling and let them know of your specific plans. We had forgotten to notify them about previous travels and had a transaction denied when trying to make a purchase internationally. Avoid the headache and embarrassment of having to put all your grocery items back in your cart at a foreign check-out counter while you are trying to contact your credit card company to straighten things out. Alert them with all of the confirmed countries you will be visiting and update the list throughout your journey.

That Ain't Me! – Fraud Alert

Traveling internationally always exposes you to potential credit card scams. Before we left, I set up a FREE one-year fraud alert on all our credit cards. You can easily accomplish this by calling Equifax's automated system at (800) 525-6285 and report that you suspect credit card fraud. They will contact you with any suspicious activity during the one-year time period, including odd credit card purchases and/or people trying to take out new cards under your name. Save time by reporting through Equifax first and they will automatically share this information with the other two credit check companies, Experian and Transunion.

Much Gratitude, Mom and Dad – Reliable Support Back Home

It is important to have someone in your home country who can provide some back-up support during your travels. This means someone who will receive and go through your mail, make deposits into your bank, check on your home and so on. My parents were a huge resource while we were traveling, and we could not have accomplished this trip without their assistance.

Do It on the World Wide Web – Online Banking

Make certain that whatever bank you use has access to online banking. Through our bank's mobile app, we were able to make payments and deposits from anywhere at any time. Also, set up all recurring bills to be paid with your credit card or automatic payment, so you don't miss a beat while vagabonding.

You Is Smart – Register for STEP Smart Traveler Notifications

STEP is a free service which allows U.S. citizens/nationals traveling abroad to enroll with the local U.S. embassy or consulate. Through this program, you list all of the countries you plan to visit and then receive travel alerts and warnings for each region. This feature came in handy when we were in Chile and were notified that there were riots in Santiago, and when we received an air-quality alert while staying in Bangkok. Also, this timely information helped us redirect our plans when we heard about some civil unrest in Southern Thailand.

Make Sure You Are Covered – International Medical Insurance

Be aware that typical U.S.-based medical insurance does not provide coverage when you travel internationally. Therefore, you will need to select a company that covers you worldwide. We partnered with an incredible insurance broker, Expat Global Medical, which deals strictly with long- and short-term international coverage.

We were surprised to find out that the cost for international insurance was significantly less than the traditional health insurance plan we were using in the U.S. In most cases, the cost of medical care internationally is much lower than it is the U.S. Therefore, your international insurance premiums may reflect this reduced cost.

Keep in mind that many of these international providers might have unique requirements to enroll in their program. To qualify for coverage by our insurance provider, we had to guarantee residency outside of the U.S. for a minimum of 181 days per year and prove that we were beyond U.S. borders on the first day coverage began. Since we wanted coverage to start January 1, but we weren't leaving for our trip until that coming June, we went on a last-minute New Year's Eve visit to Canada to ensure we fulfilled the requirements.

Can You Hear Me Now – Cell Phones and Calling Abroad

Choosing the right phone plan before you travel is imperative in order to avoid costly phone bills. Check with your current provider to see if they have worldwide coverage. Many companies offer coverage only if you are staying in Central and South America. However, their coverage and associated fees can change dramatically when you venture overseas. Make sure you know exactly what is included and not included in your plan, or you could rack up a tremendous bill. Our family was using Sprint, so we inquired about their Open World service plan which covered us from Canada to South America. Luckily, we stayed in Central and South America the first half of the trip, so that worked out perfectly.

It is very important to set up your phone for this coverage BEFORE you leave the U.S. Call your provider and have them walk you through the steps. There are several settings you must adjust in order to get set up properly. Make certain you understand your roaming feature. If your phone is not on the right setting, you could get charged astronomical fees. We found FaceTime and Zoom calls to be the best option when calling back home.

Heading overseas, the cell phone situation was a different story because our cell phone provider did not have comprehensive coverage in Asia or Europe. We ended up buying SIM cards for our phones which provided limited data and calling abilities, so we were able to have a local phone number and avoid cell phone plan issues.

Make sure to bring your passport to the sim card store or they will not let you get a card.

We made that mistake and had to walk all the way back to the hotel to get it. Also, make certain you know your username, password and pin code for your online cell phone account; you will be asked for this information to set up a SIM card.

In addition, pack a paperclip to be able to get your SIM card out of your phone. I know this sounds silly, but we spent hours searching for a paperclip while in Medellin, Colombia. Surprisingly, there were none to be found at the front desk of our hotel or at any supermarket. What is commonplace back home is not necessarily easy to access in other parts of the world. It's a little bit of a process to get a SIM card, but it's worth it.

On another note, upgrade your phone's storage plan so you will have enough space for all the fabulous pictures and videos you will take to document your adventure. There is nothing worse than getting ready to take a photo of a once-in-a-lifetime experience like you bathing elephants in Thailand, when your phone flashes the Debby Downer message that you're out of storage.

The International Way to Communicate – WhatsApp

WhatsApp is a free app that allows you to make calls, send text messages and hold video calls via Wi-Fi or data use. I highly suggest downloading this app onto your phone, as the majority of the world uses it to communicate on a daily basis. Many businesses in other countries have their WhatsApp phone number listed as their contact info. Best of all, it's totally free to use if you are connected to a reliable data-streaming source.

The Master of Maps – Waze

Waze GPS, a navigational app, is an absolute must for world travel. While renting a car in Costa Rica, we learned about this amazing tool. We knew we would not have access to the internet throughout remote areas of the country during many parts of our excursion. The great thing about Waze is that you can enter your destination while you are still connected to Wi-Fi or cell data and then it will continue to provide directions via satellite even while you are not connected to the internet. Waze literally helped us navigate around the world, in every country, with very little error.

On many occasions, we thought Waze was sending us on a wild goose chase, only later to find out that it helped us avoid a major traffic jam. Moral of the story: Waze knows… 99 percent of the time.

Your Personal Interpreter – Google Translate

The Google Translate app is a huge savior when you are hopping around between countries. While in the app, you can choose a language to download while you have Wi-Fi. You will then be able to access translations even when you are not connected to the internet.

It's so much more convenient and takes up less space than lugging a foreign language dictionary around with you for each country that you will be visiting. For the most part, the translations on Google Translate are pretty accurate. Still, be warned, it did cause some hilarious situations. On several occasions we thought the translation said something, but we ended up leaving the recipient of our words totally baffled by our message.

One of these instances was when we were living in Chile, in the small town of Talca, for seven weeks. I wanted to return some ground coffee that I did not particularly like at the grocery store that was within walking distance of our rented apartment. So, I looked up the Spanish for, "I would like to return this," and Scott and I walked into the store to make the transaction.

I approached the counter and eloquently stated my request. The gentleman and woman behind the desk looked at me funny, so I repeated it again. Then they began nodding their heads up and down like they understood what I was trying to communicate. While the woman was seemingly processing my return, I was distracted by the man who excitedly engaged us in a conversation about the U.S. and his curiosity as to why, out of all the places to venture in Chile, we had chosen the tiny city of Talca to visit.

As we were finishing our conversation, the woman turned to me with a smile and handed me back my coffee beautifully swaddled in wrapping paper with a bow. She misunderstood and thought I wanted an open package of coffee gift-wrapped! We had a good laugh while I tried to further explain my point. I guess messages just get lost in translation sometimes!

Play that Funky Music – Digital Music Downloads

It is inevitable that at some point on your trip, you will find yourself on a long plane, train or car ride. You'll want to have access to some good tunes. By that point in your travels, you might be craving some songs in English or your native language. You reach for your Pandora or Spotify music app and uh-oh… it no work-y! You fumble for your preferred playlists on your phone and realize that the same 100 songs, played over and over again for a whole year, might turn listening to your favorite tracks into absolute torture.

Unfortunately, that was a situation we experienced during our journey. There are only so many times you can hear Billy Joel's *Piano Man* before you want to bang your head on the dashboard. So, to prevent this agony, BEFORE you leave the U.S., download all your beloved rhythms from Spotify, Pandora or other music apps and store them to your phone, so you will have access at any time. Again, upgrading your phone's storage capacity to allow room for your music makes a difference. Believe me, it's worth a little effort to compile a variety of music and will do your ears a huge favor.

Head of the Line Please – Global Entry and TSA PreCheck

If you plan to re-enter into the U.S. several times throughout your venture, getting Global Entry or TSA PreCheck may save you some time in airport lines.

∿

So, as you can see, there are just a few itty-bitty things you need to do BEFORE you leave for your grand escapade. Still, believe me, it's worth investing the time doing it prior to your departure, when you have access to familiar resources. It's a whole different story trying to get the same things accomplished when you are in a foreign country, where you do not speak the language and you have spotty Wi-Fi. Putting in the effort now is like giving a fabulous gift to your future self.

∼

Key Things to Consider

- *Develop reliable support back home.*
- *Register for the STEP Smart Traveler Program.*
- *Make sure your medical insurance covers you internationally.*
- *Research the best cell-phone communication.*
- *Download useful apps like Waze, Google Translate and Spotify.*
- *Check into Global Entry and TSA PreCheck offerings.*

9

YOU MEAN I CAN GO ANYWHERE?

HOW TO CHOOSE YOUR ROUTE

"Oh, the places you'll go." – Dr. Seuss

When the Goyette family set out for our big adventure, there were 193 formally recognized countries that existed on the planet. Of course, we wanted to experience all of them. Yet, a year goes by very fast. We had to develop some kind of logical course that would weave together our desired destinations in the most cost-effective, timely manner. Still, how to choose where to go when there are so many incredibly interesting places in the world to explore?

We started the vision for our itinerary with each of us stating a few places that we then put on the "MUST SEE" list. For Kayla, it was Tokyo, Paris and London, in that order. As you may have realized, she is definitely a city girl. For Scott, he wanted to delve into Patagonia, Thailand, and Colombia to satisfy his beach and adventure preferences. Now, my country requests were a little more general. Thailand had been calling my name for years, so that made the top of my favorites. I wanted to learn Spanish while abroad, so I suggested living in some Spanish-speaking countries like Costa Rica, Guatemala and Colombia for a while. In addition, I desired to investigate Eastern Europe and discover more about my heritage in Austria and Hungary.

We did not map out every destination for the entire year we planned to be gone; we wanted to leave plenty of freedom to redirect our path based on a random suggestion from a stranger we haphazardly met along the way, or a national celebration we just had to experience. We yearned to be free of rigid timetables yet we did want to create a journey that would flow naturally as much as possible. We considered seasonal weather, off-peak times for cheaper rates and countries that offered a great value. To ignite the wanderlust inside of you, I will share a summary of our route, the reasons why we chose our path and some of the remarkable highlights from our trip. Let's get started!

Costa Rica – The Pura Vida Way of Life

Our desire was to enjoy each nation during the best possible weather. Since we were leaving for our big escape in June, we chose Costa Rica as our starting point for several reasons. Scott and I were teaching a yoga retreat there in July and had visited the country with Kayla several times prior. That meant our familiarity with the locals would be the perfect way to ease into our newfound way of life. It also gave us several weeks to explore new areas that we had not seen on previous excursions.

The weather in Costa Rica in June and July is wonderful because the jungle is lush and blooming during their green season. During this time of year, it typically rains in the evenings, leaving beautiful sunny days to spend lounging on a beach or hiking a volcano. Costa Rica being our first stopover also inspired a six-month stretch of living in Spanish-speaking countries to acquire the language.

Ultimately, we chose to investigate Central and South America during the first half of our year-long trip. Staying within a similar time zone made it an easier transition to our new mobile life and nomadic working style. We would only have one new language to deal with and could focus on absorbing as much local conversation as possible. Furthermore, we had selected to travel during non-peak seasons to reduce costs.

Arriving at the magical Anamaya Resort in the small town of Montezuma in Costa Rica to teach our ninth annual yoga retreat was like coming home to family. We were received with open arms by all the welcoming staff who had become our friends over the years. Kayla was also excited because one of her best friends, Mia, and her mom, Summer, were going to be attending the retreat. Having a good friend meet up with us at the beginning helped Kayla with her transition into our new life. I was so glad that Summer and my other great friends, Laura and Lita, joined us and were there to share the start of our trip. We spent seven high-vibe days enjoying a tropical paradise where the jungle meets the ocean.

At the end of the week, we said goodbye to our dear friends and headed towards the northern part of the country, in the Guanacaste region near the border of Nicaragua. We stayed at Dreams Las Mareas, a luxurious all-inclusive resort, practically for free through my participation in a yoga exchange program. It was wonderful to finally relax and unwind after the months of intense preparations for our global journey.

We spent a few more weeks exploring surfing villages like Dominical and Nosara. By the end of our month-long excursion, my family of three had fully embodied the simple Costa Rican way of life which they call "Pura Vida" meaning the pure life.

Then it was time to hit the road or, more accurately, the sky. We delivered our farewells to this blissful country and continued onward.

Panama – Some Like It Hot

After exploring different regions of Costa Rica for a month, we took a quick 2.5-hour flight to Panama City for a short stopover to relish in the hot Latin vibe and bright colors of this vibrant city. The Panamanian capital is an easy transition into the vagabond lifestyle if you are coming from the U.S. because there is a huge American presence, and many people speak English. The exchange rate is also simple because it's dollar for dollar and American money is widely accepted

We had the best time experiencing Casco Viejo, the Old City, with its lively ambiance and historic essence. In the evenings, we sat at vivacious cafes on the square listening to musicians strumming Latin tunes on Spanish guitars while sipping Seco-infused cocktails (a sweet national liquor) with a warm breeze blowing through the cobblestone streets. These moments felt dreamlike as Scott and I would exclaim in disbelief, "This is our life!"

Colombia – From Coffee to Graffiti, Art Encompasses Everything

We hopped on a brief two-hour flight to Medellin, Colombia where we fell in love with the stunning beauty of this valley town encircled by regal mountain peaks. We took a gondola up to Arvi Park and arrived at a gorgeous mountain nature space with lots of hiking trails. We stopped off at a farmers' market at the top of our ride and enjoyed local cuisine like *ajiaco*, a hearty chicken soup, and freshly made *arepas* – ground maize dough stuffed with a variety of delectables.

We spent three weeks in Colombia exploring other areas like the animated and historical city of Bogotá, where we were served cappuccinos with the fanciest frothy designs by award-winning baristas. We ventured through the streets of the city to observe the stunning and expressive graffiti art of its residents. Of course, we could not miss Bogotá's famous Sunday Market and Ciclovia, a weekly event where miles of city streets are shut down so that bicyclists can roam and locals can show off their dogs dressed in the most eccentric costumes. We loved wandering among endless street vendors selling the most bizarre products like snail jelly.

We also had the pleasure of being stranded on an island in the middle of nowhere, off the Pacific coast of this country for eight days without electricity, fresh water or food. But that's a whole other story to be told in the chapter "Mistakes to Avoid Along the Way".

Argentina – A Wine-Lover's Dream

We flew more than 4,000 miles down to the very bottom of the South American continent just as the Southern Hemisphere's winter was exiting. We stayed in a small apartment in the center of Mendoza, Argentina, the heart of the wine country, which is best known for their Malbecs, a variety of rich red wine. We took a leisurely drive through the countryside to discover some of the most stunning vineyards and wineries where we sampled the finest wines for mere pennies on the dollar.

Kayla even had the opportunity to take a private cooking class with a world-famous chef where she learned how to make homemade brick oven pizza. She was gifted an embroidered apron with the restaurant's logo, a bottle of locally produced olive oil and an extensive lunch – all for just $10.00. If you are looking for value, Argentina is the place to go!

Chile – Land of the Warmest, Welcoming People

We spent several months exploring the geographically long and thin country of Chile, starting with the eclectic capital city of Santiago. This was not my favorite place on the list of towns we had explored due to its extensive air pollution and high rate of theft in the area. However, there were some redeeming qualities to this city in a valley surrounded by the Andes Mountains. We enjoyed exploring numerous parks scattered across the urban plains and checking out the iconic Virgin Mary monument over-looking the town on top of the Cerro San Cristobal.

In Chile, we wanted to experience the life of the locals and decided to settle down for seven weeks in the quaint rural town of Talca. It was located a few hours south of Santiago, at the edge of the wine country, farmlands and mountains. The residents were shocked to see these tall American strangers show up in the middle of their tiny hamlet and word spread quickly about our arrival. Even Kayla, at 11-years-old, towered over the majority of adults in the area. My six-foot four-inch husband was a giant among them.

We found ourselves instantaneously being the center of attention as people pulled over in their cars to get a glance at the colossal foreigners strolling through a park or jogging on a running trail. To the locals, it was a phenomenon to see Americans venturing this far south, the opposite end of the planet, and choosing their sleepy town out of all the other famous and exciting places in Chile to stay for a while.

We were often approached on the streets and in the grocery stores by curious but friendly citizens who wanted to engage in conversation as we were easily recognized as out-of-towners. Restaurant-owners, shopkeepers and farmers' market attendants would all make mindful efforts to strike up conversation in the hope of finding an answer to the same burning question: why did we choose Talca?

To each query we would respond that we wanted to be in an

area where we could experience the genuine lifestyle and culture of this unique and vast country. That answer would always prompt a huge grin filled with pride and a warm embrace or handshake. Best of all, we would more often than not receive an invitation to their house to share an authentic, home-cooked Chilean meal with their family.

But there is a simpler reason as to why the Goyettes ended up in the little-known town of Talca. A couple of months prior to leaving the U.S., Scott had been working at a coffee shop down the street from our Austin home. A guy sitting next to him struck up a conversation about the "Go Love Now" sticker Scott had on the back of his computer, which represented the benevolent company my husband had founded.

After a few minutes of conversation explaining the phil-anthropic program that Scott developed to teach kids about self-love, compassion and kindness, Josh introduced himself and slid his chair over to Scott's table to talk some more. The exchange led to Scott telling him about our upcoming trip around the world. Josh mentioned that he had moved himself and his young family down to a small town in Chile to start a business venture, suggesting we should check out that city if we were ever in the area.

Little did we know that this chance conversation would lead us to one of the most fulfilling growth opportunities on our adventure. Although there were many challenges in trying to live in a town where the majority of the people only spoke Spanish, we were forced to quickly expand our ability to speak the local language.

A few days before we headed to Talca and got situated in our apartment, I posted a note on a Talca community website inquiring about any children's enrichment programs being offered in the area. Shortly after, I received a response from a lovely woman and her husband who owned an organic blueberry farm outside of town.

Rebecca and her family invited us over for *onces*, an afternoon tea enjoyed by Chileans. We graciously accepted the invitation and found ourselves dining on a huge spread of homemade pies, breads and jams as we sipped tea and admired their gorgeous country view of the mountains. It was wonderful to meet this kind family within the first few days of our arrival. Kayla and their daughter were the same age and hit it off right away. I felt relieved that Kayla had made a friend which seemed that it might be impossible as we were jumping from place to place. And, bonus, this welcoming family also spoke English, so we could relax when we were visiting with them!

Our apartment was two blocks away from a community recreation center that offered free yoga classes. Attending my first class, I introduced myself to the instructor in broken Spanish and explained that I was from the United States and also taught yoga.

The teacher, Paula, who is one of the kindest people I've ever met, introduced me to all the yogis. Before I knew it, she had invited me up to teach the class in Spanish! The attendees were ecstatic to be led by someone from the U.S. and they were very compassionate as I struggled to incorporate my limited vocabu-lary into the session. Afterwards, they eagerly ran up to thank me and waited in line for a chance to snap a selfie with an American yoga teacher. I felt like a movie star!

My family and I were immediately invited to an endless number of *onces*, dinners, happy hours, and we had several offers to take us on a tour of Talca. Paula and two other incredible ladies from class, Irma and Lucy, took us under their wings and asked us to explore the nearby mountain and coastal towns with them.

While in Talca, we reunited with Josh (from the coffee shop in Austin) and his big-hearted wife, Diane, who generously lent us their truck for the duration of our stay, so we had wheels to venture around town and take road trips outside the city. They gave us tips on where to find the most fresh and affordable produce, and even directed us when we needed to see a doctor.

My brother, Gregg, had introduced us to his friends, Sylvia and Igor, who coincidentally also resided in the tiny hamlet of Talca. They generously invited us over for *asado*, a traditional Chilean barbeque, where we connected with them and their sociable friends. Igor invited us to spend the weekend at their lake house in the country and even enticed us to live at their apartment for a week for free while they were out of town. Perfect timing, as we needed a place to stay when our rented apartment lease came up.

The night before our final stay in this humble province, I

offered to teach a Yogic Blindfold Dance class as a gift to all the people who had made our stay so comforting. I invited everyone we had met over the past weeks to participate in this non-traditional practice. To my great surprise, more than 30 people showed up from this conservative town for the unique experience and to say their farewells to the American family.

After seven weeks of assimilation into the community, it was such a surreal feeling to be standing in the middle of this beautiful group of blindfolded dancers, surrounded by all the incredible people who had so deeply touched our lives. It was wonderful to feel totally welcomed and we were so grateful to have been a part of the Talca community.

And that is where an "accidental" (or what I prefer to call a serendipitous) meeting at a coffee shop can lead you! As you can see, it is worth being open to receive every fleeting connection or chance meeting while you travel, as it just may lead you to the opportunity of a lifetime.

After being fully embraced by the residents of this quiet town and treated like rock stars, we headed to the very southern tip of the continent and engaged in a once-in-a-lifetime experience in majestic Patagonia. Our visit was timed perfectly to avoid the peak-season crowds; we arrived in October, at the beginning of the Chilean spring and during the first opening week of this snow-bound region.

Scott found an incredible deal staying at The Singular, a distinctive five-star hotel in Puerto Bories, on the coast in the Antartica Chilena Region. The property has a very unique history. Once housing the largest mutton-processing facility in South America, it had been transformed into a stunning, first-class extravaganza. Our accommodations included gourmet breakfast, dinner and two guided tours of Torres del Paine National Park.

We hiked some of the most stunning trails and took a break for lunch to dine on a delicious Chilean feast, surrounded by towering mountains. The shades of blue were like nothing I had ever seen before and the glacier lakes were so pristine you could not tell where the sky ended and its reflection in the water began. It was an unforgettable experience that will forever be etched into my mind.

Guatemala – Culture (and Coffee) at Its Finest

After our two-and-a-half-month stay in Chile, we flew an extensive 5,700 miles north to Guatemala to teach another yoga retreat and arrived on the mystical shores of Lake Atitlan at the gorgeous Villa Sumaya in the beginning of November. We met up with a group who had newly arrived from the U.S. and it was so wonderful to see familiar faces and meet new friends after traveling for five months. We engaged in ancient Mayan rituals including a cacao ceremony and a fire ceremony lead by an indigenous shaman. We fully immersed ourselves in the delicious local cuisine, customs and culture.

Kayla's birthday was quickly approaching at the end of November. She was feeling lonely and wanted to share the celebration with her besties from home. Luckily, my good friend, Lisa, was longing to explore Guatemala with us and had time to take off during the Thanksgiving break. I coordinated for Lisa to fly down with one of Kayla's best friends, Katherine, whose family was originally from Guatemala.

My daughter was in heaven to reconnect with her friend. We celebrated Kayla's 12th birthday in Guatemala City at the fancy open-air mall of Cayala, eating crêpes, ice cream and candy and playing on all the rides. Who would have thought Kayla would commemorate her big day in Guatemala with one of her besties by her side? Sometimes all the stars align, and magic happens!

We met up with Katherine's grandmother, who lives in Guatemala City, and we all headed to Antigua, a small historic UNESCO city surrounded by volcanoes and coffee plantations. Lisa and I went on a coffee plantation tour and it felt so good to escape with a friend for a time and do our own thing. The tour turned out to be one of the highlights of our trip. We were led through the entire process, from bean to cup, by a local farmer who was part of a co-op that helps support the coffee industry in the area. We ended the tour back at the farmer's home where we roasted and ground the coffee beans. After, I enjoyed the finest cup of coffee that I have ever tasted.

Katherine has an aunt who owns a gorgeous second home within the walls of downtown Antigua. She graciously lent us her fabulous pad while we were in town. That evening, while the girls were playing, Scott, Lisa and I sat on the rooftop deck relishing in the flavors of a local wine and gazing at the lush green slopes of the surrounding volcanoes as the sun set.

Suddenly, Scott noticed a huge puff of smoke in the distance, shooting up into the sky from the top of a peak.

"I think that volcano just erupted!" he exclaimed.

Lisa and I denounced the whole event until we started observing the glow of lava flowing down the sides of the volcano. We had just witnessed another once-in-a-lifetime experience, the eruption of Volcán de Fuego!

Katherine's grandmother seemed calm as we were a safe distance away. So, we spent the rest of the evening on the roof sipping wine, listening to the sounds of the jungle with the glow of Volcán de Fuego as our backdrop. Surreal!

Costa Rica – A Family Reunion

After saying a difficult goodbye to our friends in Guatemala, we returned to Costa Rica, this time for my brother and sister-in-law's wedding. Yes, life goes on while you are vagabonding, so you may have to weave your arrangements around family gatherings and other events as you maneuver through your travels. Luckily, Costa Rica is one of our favorite destinations and provided some much-needed engagement with family and friends to energize my clan. It was delightful to see relatives for the first time in months and the celebration immediately revitalized us.

United States – The Holidays at Home

After the big wedding party, we headed home to Austin, Texas to spend two weeks with family and friends over the holidays. Wow! Six months of vagabonding under our belts had flown by as quick as that!

If you are traveling with kids for a year or longer, I highly recommend weaving some home-base time into your itinerary midway through your excursion. Although we did not have our own house to stay in, coming back to a familiar city where everyone spoke our native language and being surrounded by much missed friends and family provided a huge opportunity to reset. In addition, it helped us gather the energy necessary to continue on the second half of our journey.

The other advantages were that we could restock on supplies that we could not find during our travels and were able to leave behind some space-wasting items we never ended up using. The short reprieve gave us an opportunity to sift through six months of mail and catch up on important bills, like paying our taxes.

We really had no idea of the route we would take for the next six months of our adventure but while we were resting at home, Scott discovered an incredible deal flying on United Airlines to Thailand in first class Polaris seats with fully reclining beds and our own entertainment pod. Yes! As a bonus, we realized we could have a five-day layover in Japan, which would enable us to check Tokyo off the list for Kayla. We booked our ticket to leave on New Year's Day to meet the "must be out of the country on the first day of coverage" requirement from our medical insurance provider.

After two weeks of having fun with her friends and being smothered with love by family, it was hard for Kayla to leave for the second half of our trip. Scott and I were excited for our first-time exploration of Asia; admittedly, we were also a little nervous to venture to cultures that were so foreign to us, with languages and customs of which we had no understanding. But I guess that is all part of the adventure.

Japan – Masters of the Washroom Experience

Arriving in Tokyo was like landing on a different planet. Every one of our senses was overloaded with exotic stimuli that rocked our brains. We tasted the strangest foods, saw the wackiest sites, and heard the most foreign sounds. Japanese letters swirled around us like we were floating in a bowl of foreign alphabet soup and we could not understand a single word.

We immediately dove into the culture and had to adapt to Japan's unique customs. Everything was a truly bizarre experience, and it was challenging to absorb it all at once. Add to that the tremendous time difference and jet lag and we were faced with the perfect storm to feel overwhelmed.

Nonetheless, once we made it past the shock of such an extremely different society, we fell in love with Tokyo. Kayla was totally enamored by the bright colors, wacky foods and "pet cafes" (themed coffee shops that provide an opportunity to hang out with a variety of animals like cats, dogs, hedgehogs and more) located up and down Harajuku Street. Although the city housed the largest concentration of people I had ever seen crammed into one place, the dense crowds were very orderly and cordial. Everyone knew exactly what to do and showed extreme respect for one another. The streets and trains were also spotless.

Above anything else, my favorite thing about Japan was their toilets. Hands down, the Japanese provide the best bathroom experience on the planet. As you plop your bum down on a warmed toilet seat, your hand rests on a remote control with a slew of buttons. You try your luck at one of them and it turns on some soothing music. You push a different button and it shoots a gentle spray of warm water at your rear-end, another sends a spray to your frontal area. Finally, an additional button gently blow dries your nether regions with balmy air. Who knew going to the bathroom in both private and public restrooms could be so absolutely wonderful? I spent as much time as possible on the bowl during our short but entertaining stay in Tokyo!

Thailand – The Land of Smiles and So Much More

We hightailed it out of Japan after five days. The prices were astronomical, and we knew we would blow all the money that we had designated for the month if we stayed any longer. After hopping on a flight to Thailand, we landed in the chaos of Bangkok, and immediately felt so grateful to have had our first introduction to Asia on the orderly, comparatively quiet streets of Tokyo. The capital city of Thailand was the extreme opposite of our experience with the reserved Japanese culture.

The number of people in the streets was astounding. What made it worse was there was no rhyme or reason to the vehicle or pedestrian traffic. It was a free-for-all with motorcycles and tuk tuks (tiny, open-air, motorized vehicles) zig zagging between cars and people on the street. Commuters were so crowded into trains that their faces were pressed against the glass windows and they fell out of the cars when the doors opened.

Now THIS was overwhelming.

We hid out in the hotel for five days, scared to leave our

room. Was *this* really the Thailand that had been calling to me for years? I had visualized myself praying in an ornate Buddhist temple high on a mountain with the view of a tropical landscape below me. I was so disappointed in the opposite reality that confronted me now.

After a few days of cowering in my room, while Scott and Kayla relaxed back at the hotel, I mustered up the courage to go explore this immense city on my own. I was so relieved at what I discovered. The residents were some of the friendliest people in the world. The spices and flavors of the local cuisine were outstanding, and everything was ridiculously cheap. A meal on the street would cost $1–3 and you could get a full hour-long Thai massage for less than $10. Score! We stayed for two months and lived like kings and queens.

Our long stint provided the opportunity to explore other cities, country villages and beach towns that all took our breath away. By the way, yes, I did fulfill my dream of praying in a sacred Buddhist temple on top of a mountain under the glow of a full moon with a view of the lush jungle below. The experience was absolutely surreal.

I am so grateful I did not give up on Thailand based on my first impressions of Bangkok. Word to the wise: the capital city of a nation is NOT always representative of the entire country. This is all the more reason to explore other regions to comprehend the full vibe of the country and get an authentic experience of its culture.

We ventured to Chang Mai in the northern highlands and had the most magical experience bathing and feeding elephants on a preserve. Make sure to do your research, as some of these self-proclaimed preserves do not treat the animals well. If you see elephant rides advertised, run away, as they severely hurt the animals.

I highly recommend signing up for a Thai cooking class in Chang Mai. It was a huge climax of our trip. For the low cost of $30 per person, we went on a tour of the local fresh markets to see all the ingredients we were going to use in our class, then we went back to an outdoor kitchen and created a five-course meal that we dined on at the end of the evening. It was fabulous!

One day, we ventured on the windiest mountain road I have ever been on. Our goal was to explore the bohemian town of

Pai, and I am so ecstatic that we did! The town has such a cool vibe and is significantly smaller than many others we visited, so it felt more authentic. Our favorite part was the night markets, where the streets came to life with vendors selling exotic and delicious cuisine for just a couple of dollars per delightful snack. We indulged on every culinary pleasure and got massages daily for just $7 per hour – we lived very large during our stay there.

We also made it down to the southern coast, all the way to Phuket, to enjoy the crystal-blue water of the Indian Ocean and have some relaxing downtime for a week after having been in sightseeing mode for so long. Phuket is an interesting town; it is family friendly during daylight hours but has a very weird undertone once the sun goes down. Countless massage parlors by day would quickly turn into sketchy places of business by night. People from around the world ventured there to get "boom boom" (if you know what I mean). We found that situation in a lot of places throughout the country, but setting that aside, Thailand did not disappoint!

Vietnam – Party Like a Rock Star

We used Bangkok as our home-base to take a couple of cheap and easy flights and explore additional Southeast Asian countries. On a whim, the Goyettes ended up in Hanoi, Vietnam where, unbeknownst to us, we arrived just a couple days before their New Year's celebrations. We welcomed in the Vietnamese New Year by indulging in appetizers and champagne, then enjoyed the view of partygoers and fireworks from the rooftop of a fancy restaurant overlooking Hoan Kiem Lake in downtown Hanoi.

In any other place in the world, we would never have been able to afford or even secure a reservation for such desirable accommodations at the last minute. However, the entire extravagant evening, including food, drinks, attendee gifts and front-row seating to witness all the festivities was only $17 per person! One drink in New York City costs more than that on a regular day, let alone at the biggest gala of the year.

Cambodia – Outstanding History, Cuisine and Customer Service, All for a Dollar

Our family had a similar delightful experience in Siem Reap, Cambodia, where the meals were tantalizing, the customer service was excellent, and everything was cheap, cheap, cheap! We stayed in a gorgeous, highly rated hotel called Royal Angkor Resort. They found out I was celebrating my birthday during our visit and brought me a birthday cake on three separate occasions! Scott commemorated my 46th trip around the sun by buying me a deluxe spa package, which included a facial, massage, gourmet lunch and afternoon tea for only $39! That birthday party will go down in the history books as one of the best.

Through our hotel, we hired an incredible guide to take us on a private tour of Angkor Wat, an ancient Buddhist complex and the largest religious monument in the world. If you are looking to explore significant archeological relics, this breathtaking complex by far surpassed any other ancient historical site we visited in its size and beauty, including the Pyramids, the Parthenon and Machu Picchu.

All of our Cambodian experiences were so cost effective they felt almost free. Southeast Asia makes your money go for miles and miles. Not surprisingly, it was hard to leave a region where we enjoyed the luxuries of royalty, dining on the finest dishes, indulging in daily massages and engaging in the most extraordinary events.

Sri Lanka – One of Our Favorite Places on Earth

We left a lot of wiggle room for flexible travel plans and decided to head to Sri Lanka based on a suggestion from a "friend" whom Scott had met through Facebook. We were so happy that we made that choice. I can safely say that Sri Lankans might just be the friendliest people on the planet – we found that strangers came up to us everywhere we went to purposely engage in meaningful conversations.

This island is the epicenter of the entire world's spice production, where they grow more than 200 different varieties. Therefore, the regional food practically jumps off the plate with an abundance of magnificent flavors and colors. Another bonus: the customer service there was second-to-none compared to the other countries we visited.

We had the pleasure of staying at a five-star Marriott Resort in Weligama Bay, at the southern tip of the country. The superior customer service made it one of our most favorite experiences of our entire journey. The local staff invited our family to partake in a private cooking class with their chef where we learned how to create curries and egg-hopper sauces using all of their vibrant spices. We also took a private helicopter tour over the Indian Ocean to spot majestic blue whales breaching the water.

We arrived in Sri Lanka at the end of February and had timed our visit to this beautiful destination perfectly – right after monsoon season and immediately before tourist season – so the weather was gorgeous and the crowds on the beaches were minimal. Weligama Bay made the list of our top favorite places in the world. Better yet, our penthouse suite hotel accommodations overlooking the ocean were 100 percent free, using a minimal number of our previously accumulated Marriott points.

I am not saying this to brag about our exquisite experience. I am stating this to make it absolutely clear that there are places in the world where you can reside in the most lavish surroundings for practically no coinage. You just have to be willing to investigate a little time and turn your travel planning into a fun game of awesome deal discoveries.

Dubai (The United Arab Emirates) – Culture and Carnival Wrapped Up into One

Next, we headed off to Dubai to experience a few days of the Muslim culture in and around the city. During prayer time, we stood along one of the many waterways of Sharjah, Dubai's conservative neighboring city, and heard the sounds of the *muezzin* calling the faithful to prayer coming from every direction, the singing echoing through the streets. What a unique and foreign sound to my ears.

I was so glad to experience and expose Kayla to the Islamic religion and to Arab culture, which was so unfamiliar to us and had so often been depicted as menacing in many American movies and books. I will admit that the *taqiyah* caps on the men and *burqa*s that many women wore were a little intimidating at first. However, just like anywhere else in the world we visited, the engagement of the local residents made me realize that, ultimately, we are all the same: everyone wants to have happiness and health for themselves and their families.

It was Scott's birthday while we were in Dubai and to celebrate, he requested we take a Jeep tour of the Arabian Desert. Although Kayla was a little nervous, we all agreed to go, as the birthday boy had all the power on his special day. We hopped in a vehicle with four other people. Our guide had deflated the tires slightly for better traction on the sand. He started the engine and began a casual ride into the desert. Suddenly, out of nowhere and to our surprise, we were flying over dunes like we were on *The Dukes of Hazard*! Within seconds, a mellow drive through this arid region had turned into a full-on death-defying adventure.

As the jeep caught air leaping above banks and slid sideways propelling over hills, Scott was able to capture a video of our three very different reactions: he laughing hysterically with the thrill of adrenalin pumping through his veins, me screaming at the top of my lungs with exhilaration and pure panic, hugging a complete stranger sitting next to me, and Kayla with an emotionless, deadpan face, seething with fury inside at the intentionally inaccurate and downscaled description of the adventure that had been provided by her father before the event.

Dubai is packed with tons of world-record marvels. We visited the Burj Khalifa, which is the tallest building in the world, towering at 2,717 feet above the earth. We stopped by the Mall of the Emirates, one of the biggest malls on the planet, to witness the phenomenon of indoor skiing at Ski Dubai. By the way, American malls cannot hold a candle to the fun-filled, carnival-like atmosphere of the malls in Dubai and Thailand. I am not a mallrat, but they are an absolute must-see!

Egypt – A Heartbreaking Disappointment

On our way to Israel, Scott booked a whirlwind tour of the Pyramids in Egypt with a quick, less-than-24-hour stopover in Cairo. Our brief stint made me feel like Chevy Chase in the movie *National Lampoons European Vacation*, when the family zips by iconic monuments in a London roundabout while announcing "Big Ben! Parliament!"

Compared to all the other majestic historical and archaeological sites on the planet, the Pyramids fell short of my "Must-See" list. Although the Pyramids themselves are one of the Wonders of the Ancient World, my view is based on the extremely depressed environment around the Pyramids and the overbearing, pushy vendors who solicit tourists to take rides on crippled camels or horses with wounded legs.

First impressions last a lifetime, and I was saddened to see children playing on garbage piled high in the streets and sickened by how poorly the animals were treated in Cairo. I was grateful for our brief stay and could not wait to leave. That being said, I will reflect back on my previous statement that the capital of a country is NOT representative of a nation. Therefore, I am open to discovering more of this country's beauty in the future.

Turkey – A Majestic Experience

Continuing on our way to Israel, Scott found an incredible deal for first-class tickets on Turkish Airlines with a 16-hour layover in Istanbul. The package included a premier tour of this beautiful city during the transit, all of it free and sponsored by the airline.

Turkish Airlines provides THE BEST first-class encounter I have ever experienced. After enjoying an authentic Turkish breakfast in a quaint local restaurant, we were whisked away on a guided tour of some of the most gorgeous mosques and palaces in the city. Followed by a delicious lunch, we were transported back to the airport and invited to dine in the most supreme airport lounge I have ever entered.

We sampled every Turkish delight you could imagine from the endless buffets and then had a relaxing massage. We even cuddled up for a nap on a comfortable bed in one of their resting rooms. I was so disappointed when they called us for our flight – I never wanted to leave. I will definitely make efforts to explore more of this beautiful, exotic country.

Israel – Family, Faith and Festivities

I was so excited to make it to Israel to meet up with my cousin Zach, his wife Stefanie and their baby. They live just outside of Tel Aviv and it was so wonderful to see familiar faces and relax with them. We had the opportunity to observe Shabbat with them by dining on a special meal on Saturday that they had prepared the night before.

We then ventured up to Jerusalem to visit the four religious quadrants of this holy city and just happened to arrive during Purim, a fun-loving Jewish holiday. It is celebrated to honor the saving of the Jewish people from Haman, an evil official of the Persian Empire. We dressed in funny clown costumes and made our way to the streets to celebrate with the rest of the locals by eating lots of candy and getting drunk.

No matter what your religious beliefs, if any, the Old City of Jerusalem houses a spiritual energy that I have no words to describe. The religious history is literally layered one on top of the other as different religious entities have conquered the area over thousands of years.

Growing up Jewish, I had always heard my grandparents talk about Jerusalem and the religious importance of the Western Wall, which is the last standing wall of the Second Temple, dating back to 19 BCE. I remember looking at the pictures my grandparents took of all the people touching the Wailing Wall during their visit to the Holy Land, and how we recited "Next Year in Jerusalem" at the close of every Passover Seder. Although I am not religious, I had to see this significant monument to honor my ancestors.

Visitors to the Western Wall are divided into two sections, one for males and one for females. Kayla, Scott and I wrote a little note of prayers and well-wishes to place in the cracks of the wall. As Kayla and I approached the large structure, we saw tens of thousands of tiny papers with messages from visitors past.

I placed my hand on the wall and closed my eyes. My mind immediately went to my grandparents and how they had touched this very same wall years before. Tears welled up in my eyes as I remembered all my descendants that had come before me and passed down the lessons, from generation to generation, that made me who I am today. It was a very emotional event that I will never forget.

Cyprus – The Island Home to the Goddess of Love

Scott found an awesome deal using points to stay at an Airbnb on the Greek side of Cyprus (Cyprus is split into two areas: Greek and Turkish) for a full week for free. We flew to this beautiful island and truly enjoyed the comforts of having a full home with kitchen for our stay. It was so fun to visit the tiny grocery store in our little village or bring produce back from the local farmer's market and prepare a meal. When you are traveling for so long, you find great appreciation in the simple things like cooking your own dinner and even doing the dishes, if you can believe it.

We rented a car during our stay to explore the entire island. We arrived in late spring, and we were able to catch the very last day of skiing on Cyprus' Mount Olympus. It was dreamlike standing at the top of the peak, surrounded by snow, viewing the Mediterranean Sea.

We also visited some wineries to sip Commandaria, the world's oldest named wine still in production. We sauntered through an olive farm where we tasted the finest olive oil and ate chocolate made from donkey milk. Along with all the fresh cuisine, we also found pleasure in conversing with the friendly locals. Cyprus was a charming and extremely economical stopover on our way to mainland Greece.

Greece – Beauty, Budget and Booze

Greece is a fabulous option right before the summer tourist season because your dollar stretches far and the crowds are minimal. You can't beat the history and nightlife of Athens. Among the modern buildings are sprinkled some of the most ancient structures in the world. We stopped by all the must-see tourist sites like the Acropolis and Parthenon, which is incredibly impressive when you consider the manpower that must have been needed to construct the temple and citadel on the highest point overlooking the city. The fact that the Parthenon is still erect after almost 2,500 years, withstanding several wars and harsh Mediterranean storms, is unbelievable!

My favorite moment in Athens was getting lost in the winding cobblestone streets and ending up at a charming coffee shop/bar, where the welcoming owner offered Kayla and me a free drink on the house. As we sipped the sweet refreshment, we slowly became giggly and began be-bopping to the uplifting tunes on the radio. When the owner came back to refill our drinks, I asked him what was in this concoction that tasted like a twist on lemonade. We were surprised to find out the main ingredient was Chios Mastiha, a Greek liqueur made from the sap of a tree found solely on the island of Chios. Kayla and I toasted our glasses, and I continued to get tipsy with my 12-year-old daughter.

We discovered delicious wineries inland and played on the gorgeous white sand beaches of the Aegean Sea an hour train ride south of Athens. I wish we had spent some time exploring the islands. Although Kayla had been a very good sport up until now, she was not up for taking the boat ride. Scott and I agreed that we would return to Greece someday to explore these magnificent islands.

Slovakia and Hungary – Back to My Roots

The Goyettes then began making our way into Eastern Europe, where we had a surprisingly good time wandering the streets of old town Bratislava, in Slovakia. From there we took a day trip on a bus up to Budapest, in Hungary, to check out the stunning river city. I was very excited for my first visit to this region because my great grandma was born there. She and her family fled to America from their homeland in the early 1900's due to anti-Semitic pogroms sweeping Hungary.

The region made me a little sentimental, as I thought of my great-grandma's story and how her feet had touched this land, even if only for a short while, as a young child. It was comforting to go to restaurants and order many of the delicious, familiar dishes that my grandma once served at her home, like potato pancakes, *kugel* noodles and dumpling soup. These were the recipes passed down from four generations in my family.

Austria – Spring is in the Air

We flew to Vienna, Austria, just in time for tulip season. Vienna is a magical city in the spring. We rented scooters and rode for miles along all of the nature trails that were mindfully woven throughout the metropolitan, stopping at coffee shops and cafes along the way. Although it's one of the more expensive urban areas of Eastern Europe, it was well worth the visit to experience the stunning gardens and historic sites.

The food there was also very soothing and familiar to me with my Eastern European roots. Kayla's worldwide search for Matzo Ball Soup (think chicken and dumplings) was finally fulfilled in Austria, where the restaurants were crammed with savory comfort foods. We celebrated Passover in another region aligned with my family heritage. We did not have time to make it to the mountains, but that will be for another trip.

Czech Republic – A Flash Back in Time

As Kayla and I were not feeling well, we hunkered down in our hotel room to rest while Scott took a day trip to the Czech Republic to expand his knowledge of Eastern European culture. He ended up in Brno, a small college town with a similar vibe to its larger sister city of Prague. This enduring European hamlet was one of the few fortunate cities to escape destruction in World War II. Therefore, it has the perfect combination of old- and new-world energy.

Like many Eastern European towns, Brno is centered around a gorgeous, open town-square which provides space to host artists, festivals and other various entertainment. As Scott explored the network of underground tunnels which were built to house war-struck citizens during raids, he experienced an overwhelming sense of the challenging conditions of the time. The Palace Hotel, built in the heart of the city during the mid-nineteenth century, is another stunning destination to encounter during your visit. Overall, the Czech Republic is an excellent value with gorgeous views, scrumptious cuisine and lots of history.

Romania – Dracula and Beyond

Heading off to Romania, we spent a few days in Bucharest. This once communist country was a very different experience to the unique and colorful landscapes of Austria. With the buildings in Bucharest looking very institutional and uniform, you could easily tell that Romania is one of the poorest countries in Eastern Europe, even though it was an advantage when it came to getting a lot of tourism value for your money.

The fighting during World War II had destroyed much of the city's original infrastructure so they made an effort to reconstruct "Old Town," which ended up being quite quaint for a modern rebuild. My brother-in-law, Paul, met up with us there for a few days. Again, it was so great to be around family and have relaxed conversations in English.

We chose to take one of the oldest and slowest trains on a four-hour ride north to Transylvania, the land of Dracula. I could practically run alongside the train and get there faster by foot. This leisurely, no-frills ride allowed us to see the countryside of Romania, and all of its rolling hills and steep, peaked mountains. We arrived in Sibui on a rainy evening and had to make a big jump off the train with all of our luggage because they did not have a proper station platform to step on.

We loved breathing the fresh air of the heavily forested town as we ventured onto the trails that meandered through the region and entered the medieval hamlet to wander around the square. We checked out the old buildings whose roofed-lined air vents looked like creepy eyes that followed you with their gaze.

Another great deal from Scott led us to a free stay at the fabulous Hilton Hotel in Sibui that included full spa services and a great local breakfast. Right next to our hotel, we were shocked to find a restaurant that served Texas BBQ. We ate there for three nights in a row, so satisfied by the comforts and familiar flavors of home. While we were dining there one night, I was surprised to hear my name being called out. I turned around to find the sister of a friend from Texas sitting right next to us. What a small, small planet we live on!

Although we did not partake, if you are interested in the folklore of Dracula, you can take a tour and follow in the footsteps of the legend from his birthplace to his final resting place. Unbeknownst to many, Dracula is actually a mythical character, but based on a real person, Vlad III, Prince of Wallachia or – as he is better known – Vlad the Impaler. He received his morbid nickname based on his taste for blood and the heinous way he disposed of his enemies.

Poland – An Enchanted Fairytale

We headed to Poland because we found an incredible bargain, again using our credit card travel points: a free two-week stay. It was a perfect opportunity to connect with Scott's roots and absorb the deep history surrounding World War II. We quickly discovered this charismatic country to be one of our favorite places on the planet.

Our clan was enamored by the medieval city of Krakow. For Scott, he immediately felt at home with all the foods he was accustomed to like pierogis, freshly-made cottage cheese and the best borscht beet soup we have ever consumed. Wawel Castle, sitting high on a hill in the center of Old Krakow overlooking the Vistula River, set the stage for a charming experience as we wandered the cobblestone streets, popping into quaint cafes to munch on snacks. This gorgeous city has the largest town square in Europe, housing artists, performers and endless cafes.

Contrasting with the stunning beauty of this fantasy-like town is the deeply engrained history of World War II. I am obsessed with historical fiction around this era and had read several books about this time period, weaving the topic into Kayla's studies, before our arrival. We walked the streets of the Jewish ghetto, an area where they forced Jews to live during the war in slum-like conditions. We learned how the Nazis forced Jews, Gypsies and native Poles into cattle trains headed for concentration camps such as Treblinka, Sobibor, Chelmno and Auschwitz-Birkenau.

Visiting Auschwitz-Birkenau, the concentration and extermination camps where 1.1 million people were tortured and killed, was one of the most emotional experiences I have ever encountered. I could barely breathe witnessing the scratch marks on the walls of the gas chambers made by thousands of naked people who were crammed into these small spaces under the presumption they were taking "a shower", only to be gassed and perish with their entire family. Words cannot express the heartache I felt imagining the trauma these people had to endure.

I mention these moving events that we learnt about on our trip to illustrate that world travel has the benefit of leading you to places to have direct connections with things you have perhaps only heard or read about in novels. No book or movie can take the place of experiencing history first-hand. It was an incredible opportunity for Kayla to get a sense of the true devastation that had occurred during this time period. I truly believe that educating children about such tragedies opens their minds and plants seeds that help prevent atrocities like this from happening in the future.

After our time in Krakow, we headed to Warsaw for a brief visit. It had a completely different energy from Krakow, perhaps because the city was nearly 100 percent destroyed during the war and the rebuild occurred during the communist era, with Soviet funding. Therefore, many of the buildings were plain in comparison to the vibrant colors of its sister city further south. Warsaw Old Town was a great attempt at the reconstruction of the beautiful city it once was.

We had the most fabulous train experience of our entire trip while heading north to the coastal town of Sopot, which resides on the Baltic Sea. We spent our days cruising on bikes and scooters up and down the boardwalk, which ran along the shore of this charming village. It was the perfect vacation spot as we arrived right before the summer tourist season to enjoy crowd-free streets. Our housing was complimentary at the magnificent beach-front Sopot Marriott Resort and Spa, once again thanks to the use of our credit card point system!

France – Macarons Anyone?

To check off one of Kayla's requested cities from our travel list, we headed to Paris for a few days to delight in a Parisian spring. Although Paris is one of my least favorite cities based on its immense cost of living and the overall low value you get for your dollar, I have to say we appreciated our time there. We hit the farmer's markets to buy fresh produce and baked goods, then headed to a park for a picnic, French-style, to snack on baguettes and brie. One of our favorite encounters was delving into a macaron pastry class with a Parisian chef where we learned how to make this infamously difficult, but delectable culinary treat.

We connected with some friends, William, Nathalie, and their kids, who lived in the area. We were so grateful when they invited us to their flat for a typical home-cooked French dinner. It felt comforting to be sitting with a familiar family at a real dinner table having a free-flowing conversation while feasting on a homemade meal. I could tell this was just the environment me and my two travel buddies needed after having spent the last few days maneuvering through the busy streets of this hectic town.

As I mentioned before, you do not get a lot of bang for your buck in this iconic city. If you don't mind spending $17 for a cup of coffee (yes, this is how much a crappy cup of coffee costs near the Eiffel Tower), then this city is for you. There are endless cities in Eastern Europe that we found to have more charm, appeal and value. However, the French countryside and coastal towns are worth exploring. For Scott and me, Paris does not make our must-see list. Nonetheless, we are glad we fulfilled Kayla's dream of eating cream puffs and croissants to her heart's content in the city that perfected the concept of dessert!

Spain – Can You Say Fabulous Sangria, Parks, and Paella

If you are looking for value in Western Europe, Spain is the place to be. We headed to the little-known resort town of Murcia in the southeastern part of the country for some much needed R & R and a change of pace after Paris. Believe it or not, hopping from place to place sightseeing takes a lot of energy. I would suggest that you build in some downtime in between your heavy tourist activities. We relaxed at the stunning resort-style Double Tree La Torre for free using our honors points and dined on tapas (appetizers) and sangria while lounging beside the pool.

Next, we headed up to Valencia and were amazed at how much this coastal metropolitan city had to offer. Among the lush parks that meander through the center of town, there are miles and miles of mindfully planned trails for pedestrians, bicyclists and scooters. The museums are centrally located and easily accessible.

Valencia's historic center was filled with cafes where you could sip sangria and delight on the famous and flavorful dish of the region, paella, a scrumptious Spanish rice dish flavored with saffron. We were pleasantly surprised by the romantic ambiance and family friendly energy of this vibrant town. Again, we used our points for a free stay and were grateful for all the cheap, indulgent experiences we encountered in this less popular tourist destination in Spain.

England – Sophisticated City and Country Appeal

We closed in on our final international stop and the last city on Kayla's wish list, London. I was so excited to land at Gatwick Airport, knowing we would soon be convening with one of my best childhood friends, Nuala, and her son Luke, who were flying in from Ireland. If you have the chance to reunite with friends along your journey, I highly recommend it. Having other people around besides your traveling partners changes the dynamics and freshens things up a bit. Although the finish line was in sight, by this point in our trip we really craved interactions with humans other than ourselves.

We chose to take a more affordable route and stay at an airport hotel outside of London, as this is another city that can eat up your dollars in a minute. Luckily, we accumulated another free stay to offset the cost of this expensive town. The five of us did a whirlwind tour of London, which included the Changing of the Guard at Buckingham Palace, Big Ben and Parliament while viewing all the iconic markers along the way. Our favorite place to hang out was Camden Market where you can delight in a wide array of cuisine while sipping on a flavorful libation of your choice. Plus, the people-watching was magnificent – we enjoyed the funky flare of the local fashions.

After London, we bravely rented a car to tour the western part of the country. I say "bravely" because Scott would be driving on the opposite side of the road, navigating from the opposite side of the car. To top it all off, we could not find an automatic vehicle, so he would be forced to shift in an unnatural manner with his left hand. Little did we know that we chose to head out on a bank holiday, when the traffic was backed up for miles. The challenge of this drive was exacerbated by the infinite roundabouts he had to maneuver through every five minutes, which seemed to take you in counterintuitive directions. Needless to say, our whole gang was screaming during the entire trip, either from fear or anger.

We followed directions using the Waze app, making a pit-stop at Stonehenge on the way to the world heritage city of Bath. A road sign said Stonehenge was THIS way, but Waze said it was THAT way. We decided to rely on Waze and yet it took us down a dirt road through someone's farm. Along with everyone else, I was beginning to lose confidence and patience after being on a two-hour road trip that had ended up lasting more than four hours.

Suddenly we rounded a curve, and there in front of us was the iconic Stonehenge. Waze had taken us a back route to avoid the tremendously long line of cars waiting to peek at the ancient site. We jumped out of the car, avoiding the lines, stared at the odd monoliths in the middle of a field for five minutes (not worth the trip) and then did a virtual wheelie out of there. Hail to Waze! I am a full believer in you, oh mighty master of the roads!

United States – "Country Roads, Take Me Home, to the Place I Belong"

After saying cheerio to our dear friends, there was only one more country to visit, the grand ole US of A! After 51 weeks exploring foreign countries, all three of us were so excited to be homeward bound. Before our final destination in Austin, we stopped off in the Boston area to pay a visit with my sister and brother-in-law, Jess and Billy. As soon as we touched down on U.S. soil, I could hear the relief in Kayla's voice and see relaxation sweep over her face. She was more than ready to enjoy the comforts of home by that time.

From the airport we immediately headed to Bill and Bob's Roast Beef Shop to indulge in a local, long-missed favorite. Then, before we hit Jess' condo, I stopped by a pharmacy store to pick up some items. I gathered all my things and headed to the checkout counter. The woman rang me up and announced that I owed her $19.58. I stood there for a moment, in shock. No foreign language to interpret. No currency exchange to try to figure out in my head. *You mean, I can just slide my credit card through the machine, and it is as simple as that?* I found myself laughing out loud, as I exclaimed, "This is so easy!" to the baffled cashier.

After relishing in all the coziness of Massachusetts, we headed south to visit my best friend, Alisa, and her family. I had not seen her in over a year and was so thrilled to connect with "my sister from a different mister." As we pulled up to their home, Alisa and her daughter Alexa ran out, dressed in red, white and blue, with flags and banners flying, singing the National Anthem to us. I could sense the weight of having my mind alert and turned on 24/7 for a whole year suddenly being lifted off me, as I fell into the ease of being surrounded by familiar sounds, smells and tastes.

Last, but certainly not least, we arrived at our final destination: Home Sweet Home. I could feel the energy of anticipation rising among the three of us as we flew over Austin's capitol building and got a spectacular view of our home city. We stepped outside the airport and breathed in the pleasant and distinctively earthy smell of Austin. Scott and I turned to each other with big smiles and breathed a sigh of relief that we made it 365 days around the world, unscathed. We did it!

As you can see, when you engage in long-term travel, the world is your oyster. The places you will explore, the unique foods you will taste, the exciting people you will meet and the adventures you will have are absolutely limitless. Whether your goal is to see as many countries as possible during your time-frame or live the local life for a season in a foreign land, you can create any experience your heart desires. Living your dream all comes down to what I like to call the "Three Basic TION's": **Imagination, Visualization and Manifestation**.

Every single thing you see in front of you has been created in this order. I'll give you an example: your dwelling. When the general contractor set out to build your home, they hired an architect to design the layout. The architect didn't just spew out an idea within seconds and hand it to the contractor. They spent time with their IMAGINATION dreaming about how your home would appear. In their mind, they saw pieces of a puzzle floating around that represented different aspects of your home: the roof line, number of bedrooms and bathrooms, the flow of the kitchen, and so on. Once they had an understanding of all the moving parts, the whole structure started to appear in their vision.

That is where VISUALIZATION took over. Now, the architect envisioned the entire home with all the details. They clearly saw the color of the structure and the flow of the layout as you enter the front door. Every feature was distinctly apparent in their mind, like it already existed.

Here is where MANIFESTATION enters the picture. Manifestation is a vision becoming reality. The architect focused on your home as a whole entity, designed the plans, passed them to the general contractor to implement their vision, and here you are today, lounging in your house reading this book. Voila!

Now back to YOUR world travel plans. Developing and implementing your voyage follows the same exact process. Don't worry about the manifestation part. If you imagine and visualize your strategy, the steps and resources *towards* manifestation will naturally appear.

I will let you in on a little universal truth: what you focus on becomes reality. Be your own guinea pig and try concentrating on your dreams. I dare you to spend a few minutes each day focusing on your passions and see where it leads you.

Imagination, Visualization and Manifestation are all it takes to make your dreams into a reality in every aspect of your life. So, go rev up that imagination!

～

Key Things to Consider

- *Leave plenty of flexibility in your travel schedule for spontaneity.*
- *Visit areas during off peak seasons for better value.*
- *Imagination, Visualization and Manifestation will make your dreams a reality.*

10

BLESSED BY A NATIVE AMERICAN CHIEF
TRAVEL SAFETY

"Life begins at the end of your comfort zone." – Neale
Donald Walsch

One month before our initial departure, Scott and I met with a Native American Chief outside of Austin to partake in a sweat lodge ceremony. It was our first time soaking up the unique energies of this powerful ritual. Our purpose was to cleanse any negative forces and release adverse thoughts that might provide virtual roadblocks during our grand escapade. As you can imagine, we wanted things to flow as smoothly as possible.

We sat knee to knee with twelve other participants, huddled in a tipi-like structure that was smaller in diameter than a round table at a wedding, with a ceiling that hovered just above our heads. The temperature in the tight space began to rise as the Chief placed one heated rock after the other into the center pit, dousing each one with water. Hot steam occupied every inch of the dome as the darkness enveloped our senses. Over the past months, I had been building up fearful thoughts about the safety of our trip: *Would people take advantage of our naïveté and try to scam us? Would we be targeted as foreigners and robbed everywhere we went? Would Kayla be stolen from us and sold to a drug lord for sex trafficking?* But this intense environment released them with a vengeance and all of these doubts popped into my mind, one after the other, like popcorn exploding in a microwaved bag. My vivid imagination continued to grow as time went on.

Suddenly, drums and chanting commenced and brought me into the present. Every beat of the tribal rhythm called me back to Planet Earth and grounded me in sensibility. Every affirmation from the Chief reconfirmed my confidence that my family would be protected while on the road. I could feel my worries yield to the glow of the stones. The magical collective energy circled around my being.

At the closing of the ceremony, Scott and I stood before the Chief as he instilled a final blessing of safety and security for our journey.

"May your journey fill your mind with wonder, may you explore the depths of your heart as you connect deeply with others on your travels and may protection surround you every step of the way."

I breathed out a sigh of relief, absorbing his words which danced around in my mind.

I fully believe there must have been some potent magic in his language, because we felt extremely protected during our entire trip. That being said, there was plenty of mindful planning that we incorporated into our travel plans and our vagabond lifestyle always centered on safety. We started our protection strategy at home while packing for our trip. Here are a few tips that might come in handy:

Less Appeal, Less to Steal – Leave Your Bling at Home

To avoid being flashy and drawing attention to ourselves, off went the wedding rings; we stored them at my parent's house for safekeeping. As mentioned before, we originally thought of bringing our Nikon camera however, on second consideration, we decided our iPhone 6s would be fine for taking pictures along the way. They were much less bulky and more inconspicuous. Leaving everything of value at home made our travels that much more relaxing because we did not have to be on constant guard.

Zip It – Selecting the Right Gear

We chose backpacks that were large enough to store everything we required but small enough to easily safeguard our belongings in crowded areas. We loved the sturdiness and expandability of our High Sierra packs.

Before our year-long departure, I usually carried a medium-sized shoulder purse to lug around all my junk. For travel, though, I did not want to expose myself to potential theft or pickpocketing. Instead, I chose the smallest cross-body purse that I could find to hold the basics, including credits cards, cash, my phone and passport.

Baggalini makes amazing, durable products that are specifically designed for effective travel. I loved that I could wear all of my important belongings under my clothes and undetected in my small Baggalini purse, and still have effortless access to my things as needed. The straps are heavy duty, so cannot easily be cut and they have lots of zippers for safe storage. Abundant zippers are key when choosing the right luggage for your trip. Luckily, we never encountered problems with bag-snatchers at any point on our journey.

Let's Do a Wheelie Out of Here! – Smart Travelers Enrollment Program (STEP)

Another thing to consider is the safety-to-risk ratio of each country you plan to visit. Some countries like Costa Rica and Thailand welcome foreigners with open arms, while other countries … not so much. We found out the atmosphere of a country can change from minute to minute.

One night in Santiago, Chile, we were exiting our apartment, which was located off the main street running through the city, when out of nowhere a huge gathering of people developed. Suddenly the police started spraying high pressure water at the group to break up the crowd! We could not understand what was happening. Scott insisted we move in the opposite direction immediately and his instinct proved to be spot-on as the event turned out to be a group of frustrated students rioting about the poor education system in the country.

As you can see, when traveling abroad, your stable environ-

ment can change in a flash. The best way to stay informed about
your potential or current location is to register under the **STEP
Smart Traveler Enrollment Program**, a free travel safety
program offered by the U.S. Department of State to all U.S. citizens. Log your dates and countries of travel and you will receive
notifications about travel advisories in each place you intend to
visit.

These warnings redirected our plans on several occasions to
safer ground but, equally, please do not let these announcements
scare you out of visiting your desired destination. They merely
provide timely information to make an educated decision. The
program designates a color based on current risk conditions for
each country ranging from green (safe to visit) to red (avoid
area). Many of the locations we explored displayed a yellow or
even an orange escalated warning. We took these notices with a
grain of salt, did our own research and moved forward from
there.

You Want Me to Downsize Even More? – Lighten Your Load

When you plan on exploring several cities and towns within a
country, it's smart to lighten your load and your exposure to theft
by keeping all non-essentials secured in one location. Scott
figured out a very effective—and free—way to do this. Upon
arriving in a new city, we typically would stay at an internationally recognized hotel brand like Hilton, Marriott or Hyatt as our
base for the first few nights exploring the town, and for the last
night before we exited the country.

Most of these well-known hotels offer a service where you
can store your luggage free of charge for several days, even
weeks, as long as you are returning to stay. Therefore, you can
slim down your possessions to a small day bag or travel pack and
leave the rest behind, worry free, while you gallivant through the
country.

Guarding Your Goods – Make It SAFE

Another thing to consider when selecting your accommodations
is to make certain that your new home has a locking safe. As an
extra precaution, most international hotels, Airbnbs and resorts

offer a safe in your room. We never had an issue with someone stealing from our lodgings, but it is better to be *safe* than sorry.

If you are going to stay in a sketchier part of town, you might consider booking an accommodation that has a security officer in the lobby as an extra safety measure. In addition to providing a layer of safety, they proved to be an excellent resource in recommending the most delicious local restaurants and fun things to do around town.

Did You Make a Purchase at *Big Betty's Bath House*? – Credit Card Protection

I have written about this previously, but it is worth mentioning again. Before we left on our trip, we hopped on the Equifax credit score website and put a credit alert on all our credit cards for a full year. If you state that you suspect credit card fraud, they will give you the credit card protection for free. To save time, register with Equifax first and the company will automatically forward your request to the other two credit agencies, Experian and Trans Union. We never ran into a problem with identity theft while traveling and I attest our luck to participating in this free service.

From Helicopter Parent to Free-Range Parent – Child Safety

When it comes to safety precautions, traveling with children elevates your awareness to a whole other level. At the beginning of our grand adventure, the two Goyette "elders" were on high alert trying to protect our most precious asset, our 11-year-old daughter, Kayla. During the initial month of travel, we did not let her leave our side. You might have called us helicopter parents as we felt the need to hold her hand every time we left the familiar surroundings of our hotel or apartment. We maintained no more than a 10-foot distance from her at all times when we were out and about.

As time wore on, however, Scott and I allowed our guard to relax a little and we began to give her more space. We really stepped back and lightened up while I was teaching yoga at an all-inclusive resort in Costa Rica. The hotel was very family friendly, but there was an adult-only restaurant that Scott and I were dying to try. Desperate for a little alone time after experiencing our family trio 24/7 for several months, we asked Kayla if she would like to stay in the room by herself and watch a movie while we went for a quick bite to eat. She gladly accepted our offer, needing a little solo time herself.

We went over all the safety rules: "If someone knocks on the door, do not say a word. Peak through the peep hole and do not open the door EVER unless it's Mom and Dad. If there is an emergency, call our phones. If for some reason you cannot reach us, dial 0 and tell the operator your room number and the problem."

"I got it, I got it!" she said with an exasperated sigh.

We kissed her goodbye, closed the door behind us and then ran around the corner and waited. We wanted to test her stranger danger skills.

After about 10-minutes, we rapped on the door, stepped out of view and awaited her response. We endured two minutes of pure silence and then the light through the peep hole went dark as she peered through the opening to identify the visitor.

"You did great!" we exclaimed and skipped off to our first date night in ages.

We enjoyed every minute of our coveted time alone. The meal was fabulous and the wine flowed as we got swept away in our romantic moment. Throughout our dinner I wondered how Kayla was doing by herself but continued to enjoy the special date with my hubby.

After dessert, we stepped out onto the veranda overlooking the ocean to find an energetic cover band playing 80s music—my favorite! I thought of Kayla up in the room all alone, but the playful buzz of the alcohol took over my senses.

"Let's stay and listen to just one song," I said, winking at Scott. One 80s hit lead to another as we bee-bopped to the groovy tunes of our era.

When the band finished their last song, I glanced at the time. Anxiously, I realized it was almost 11 pm. We had been gone for several hours! We hurried frantically up to our room, certain that Kayla would be desperately awaiting our return. We entered the suite and found our pre-teen daughter lying in the middle of the bed with her feet kicked up on a pillow, watching the movie

Ghostbusters, surrounded by plates filled with half-eaten mac-n-cheese, chicken tenders and an ice cream sundae.

"I ordered room service!" she screamed over the blaring TV. "I even got a steak for Daddy and tipped the waiter," she said, pointing to a covered plate on the table.

This girl had taken full advantage of the ALL-INCLUSIVE nature of our accommodations. At that moment, Scott and I both realized how grown-up and self-sufficient she had become since the start of our adventure.

Yes, traveling with kids puts a focus on safety concerns. It also provides an excellent opportunity for children to learn some street smarts and travel savvy.

Throughout our journey we watched Kayla's confidence soar as she led our pack across the chaotic streets of Hanoi, Vietnam. I knew she had matured when she grabbed my hesitant hand and pulled me onto an over-stuffed train in Bangkok where the passengers were smooshed in so tight that their faces pressed against the windows and people fell out of the train car when the doors opened.

As with all exploration, there should always be a balance between personal welfare and self-discovery. Vagabonding provides the chance to examine both of these aspects on a very grand scale. Check in with yourself from time to time during your travels to assess whether you have achieved that balance. Are you selecting your itinerary based on fear or wisdom? Are you relying on suspicion or intuition to guide you on your journey?

Admittedly, I caught myself leaning towards the direction of worry and doubt sporadically throughout our trip. My concerns about safety would sometimes overpower my longing for adventure. But in the end, I would release into the precious words of our Native American Chief: "May your journey fill your mind with wonder, may you explore the depths of your heart as you connect deeply with others on your travels and may protection surround you every step of the way."

～

Key Things to Consider

- *Leave ALL valuables at home.*
- *Purchase luggage with a lot of zippers and sturdy straps to keep your belongings safe and secure.*
- *Register for the STEP – Smart Travelers Enrollment Program.*
- *Choose accommodations that provide a safe to protect your valuables and documentation.*
- *Register with Experian to protect yourself from credit card fraud while you are traveling.*
- *Child safety should be a perfect balance of personal welfare and self-discovery.*

11

A LITTLE BIT OF OCD CAN'T HURT

STAYING ORGANIZED

"For every minute spent organizing, an hour is earned." –
Benjamin Franklin

Traveling to foreign lands can be a very humbling experience. Not knowing the local language is often extremely disorienting when it comes to trying to accomplish the simplest of tasks. You immediately feel like you are trapped in your two-year-old body: you know what you want to communicate, but you have no idea how. Moreover, all the resources you had once easily tapped into for the answers no longer exist.

Imagine asking a toddler to take a trip to the grocery store to pick out some food for dinner. This little being would have to figure out where they were going, find safe transportation to their destination, choose the proper ingredients, pay for the groceries and then maneuver their way back home. Sounds terrifying when you think about it that way, doesn't it? Well, that is exactly how it feels when you first arrive in unfamiliar territory where people speak a different language.

To ease angst and confusion during your journey, and keep your sanity while traveling, one of the best things you can do for yourself is to stay organized. From where you place things in your luggage to keeping a daily routine, it is imperative that you create some stability in your life while everything around you is swirling in change. This is especially so when you are traveling with children.

Here are some pro tips to add a sense of structure to a totally unstructured experience:

A True Lifesaver – Things to Know Before You Go

When traveling with others, everyone should be responsible for an assigned job throughout the entire trip. This will help you stay organized and disperse the duties among all members of your pack.

During our adventure, Scott was responsible for setting up our accommodations and transportation. Kayla was assigned the duty of researching fun things to do in the area. I was in charge of answering a list of questions that we developed along the way to help ease our transition into our upcoming destination.

I have listed, below, a few ways I prepared for each of our future destinations. If you invest a few minutes of your time responding to these lifesavers, I promise you will enjoy a more relaxed assimilation into your new world.

"Como Se Llama" – Basic Local Phrases

Learn these six basic words/phrases for every country—not only will they make your life easier, but your hosts will greatly appreciate your efforts in trying to communicate in their native language: Hello, goodbye, thank you, please, how much? Where is the… (hotel, bathroom, restaurant etc.)?

Show Me the Money – Currency and Exchange Rate

Research the name of the local currency and the exchange rate. Protect yourself from getting ripped off on your money exchange by knowing the current rate. Note that exchange rates fluctuate from day to day. Download the app *My Currency Converter & Rates* for easy access to foreign exchange rates even when you are not connected to the internet.

I Don't Get It – Cash or Credit

Find out if cash or credit is accepted by the majority of local businesses. You will discover that many street markets are cash only, while brick-and-mortar-type businesses often accept credit and debit cards.

When you arrive at the airport, always take out a little local currency in case you need money for transportation or gratuities but note that the best exchange rates are usually to be found at ATM machines. Be sure you read the fine print when you are processing the transaction. Often foreign banks try to tack-on high fees by tricking you into choosing how you want to view the conversion. Always choose to see the exchange in the local country's conversion, NOT in U.S. dollars; this will save you some extra dough.

Ride in Style! – Uber vs. Taxi

Find out if Uber is available at your destination. If so, choose it over a standard taxi. We found Uber rides to be consistently safer, cleaner, more reliable and affordable than local cabs. Also, there is something to be said about the accountability Uber places on their drivers in order to be an active employee.

In a few countries, Uber was not officially legal but there were plenty of Uber rides floating around the cities, nonetheless. During these circumstances, you may have a challenge getting an Uber ride from the airport because law enforcement heavily monitors ride-share exchange in this environment.

We realized this when we called for an Uber ride in Colombia and the driver requested that we meet him in the airport parking lot (instead of outside baggage claim) and suggested one of us sit in the front seat to act like we were friends. To protect our Uber driver, we purposely gave him a big hug and acted like we were family when he dropped us off at the airport upon our return, so we would not be suspicious to police.

Watch Out for Mr. Montezuma – Drinking the Water

This is an imperative question to research in order to escape a trip to the local hospital. In some places, you will find it is safe to drink the water in well-branded hotel chains, but not in Airbnbs.

Be certain the water is purified before you take a sip or brush your teeth with it. It may be better to stay away from consuming tap water altogether while on your journey. Every water source is loaded with local bacteria that may not upset the tummies of the native residents but could send you rushing to the bathroom with cramps and diarrhea.

Don't Clog the Bowl – To Flush or Not to Flush

And the MOST important question of all: should you flush the toilette paper? I know this query sounds like a no-brainer if you come from a "first-world" country, but you would be surprised at how many countries such as Costa Rica, Chile and Guatemala place a waste basket next to the toilet which is meant for your doody wipes. I can attest to the fact that you do not want to make that mistake and clog their delicate toilets. Scott did some doozies on our trip and it made for some very embarrassing phone calls to hotel maintenance for cleanup. Yikes!

Where in the World? – Know Your Location

During our travels, I gave myself the title of "Map Girl". Everywhere we went, I found myself hoarding local maps from hotels, visitor centers and car rental facilities. It wasn't enough to look on Waze or Google Maps to see where our accommodations were located in each city— I yearned to have a bird's eye view of our position as it related to the entire urban area. For me, being aware of my exact locale in the world helped me find my bearings and made me feel grounded.

Of course, I got a lot of slack from my two companions as I desperately tried to find a map upon arriving at each new place. They could sense my unease until I gripped that precious piece of folded paper inscribed with street names and tourist markers in my hands. Immediately, my frantic energy would subside as I figured out the exact coordinates of where my feet were touching the earth. Aaah!

In addition to providing a sense of acquaintance in unfamiliar territory, a paper map may just save the day when you find yourself lost in the middle of a strange town with no access to Wi-Fi and therefore no digital compass. In addition, pointing to the circle you made on your map to identify your hotel comes in handy when the only language you can use to communicate with the locals is sign language.

Yes, I stand by my innate urge to grasp this coveted bundle of information in my hands. Although my two buddies won't admit it, my map fetish saved our butts countless times while lost somewhere on the planet. Invest in your free copy today!

Where's My Comb? – Packing Your Luggage

When choosing your luggage for long-term travel, my mantra is the more compartments the better. As I already mentioned, investing in packing squares to keep your clothes organized is key. In addition, luggage compartments, preferably with zippers, are a great way to keep everything safely in their place. There is nothing worse than having to tear your whole bag apart looking for your hairbrush.

Choose a designated space in your luggage for all your personal items and always return them to that place. That way you can easily access everything you need throughout your voyage. Furthermore, you can avoid accidentally leaving your items behind by doing a quick check of all your compartments for their assigned articles.

Get Up, Be Amazing, Go Back to Bed – Establish a Routine

When I was a new mom, I noticed Kayla always did better throughout the day if we stuck to a routine. She would wake up, get her diaper changed, have her first feed, a little play time, catch a power nap and then start the whole thing all over again. I always tried to go with the flow of Kayla's own internal clock instead of sticking to rigid schedules. I observed that other parents who enforced inflexible timetables on their babies ended up feeling stressed and frustrated, never meeting their expectation of a perfect schedule.

In order to reduce the sense of chaos during our travels, my clan decided to incorporate a little bit of a routine (not schedule) into our daily lives. The last thing you want is stringent timelines to stress your nerves however, some predictability in your day can be tremendously grounding in an environment that is constantly changing. This is especially true if you are traveling with kids.

Here is an example of a day in the life of the Goyettes on a typical weekday during our travels:

All three of us have very different internal clocks. Therefore, I would always be the first one up, which gave me time to meditate and go for a run or walk.

Next, Kayla and Scott would rise out of their slumbers and we would make breakfast together. Then we would engage in a couple of hours of school/work time. A lunch break was next on the list. Sometimes we would venture out to a restaurant or make a snack at our current "home". Next, another hour of work/school before we would break for some kind of exercise. This might look like visiting the hotel gym, jumping rope in the living room, renting a bicycle or running on the beach.

After completing all our to-dos at around 2 pm, we would be ready to take off and explore our surroundings. We would sometimes have dinner while out on our adventure or would bring groceries back to cook at "home". Then, we would wind down the evening with games, reading or screen time. Finally, we would fall asleep whenever our bodies were ready for rest.

I relished in the fact that we never had to wake up to an alarm in the morning and did not need a wristwatch to keep us on track. We had flexibility in our routine to flow with the vibe of the day. We owned our time. That my friend is the ultimate feeling of freedom!

Making a List, Checking It Twice – A Final Sweep Through

Last but not least, here is an extremely important pro tip: To lighten the stress of jumping from place to place during your travels, always do a final sweep through of all accommodations before you move on. We learned this early on in our trip, when we left behind a precious computer charger at a hotel in Costa

Rica in the first month of our adventure. Considering our computers were literally our lifeline to work, school and staying connected with friends and family while traveling, we spent a painstaking amount of time, energy and money trying to find a replacement.

Going back to assigning everyone a job, make certain all of your travel mates are responsible for packing their OWN personal items. Then delegate one reliable member of your team to do a once-over of all closets, draws, cabinets and any other potential hiding places for your stuff before leaving your accommodations. I guarantee these efforts will save you from extensive irritation in the long run.

I hope some of these tips will make you feel more centered as you absorb all the magic, mystery and pleasure the world has to offer. A little bit of organization goes a long way and can provide that centered sensation which will propel you to soar through your adventure. Aaah…I feel grounded already!

Key Things to Consider

- *Know before you go: basic phrases, exchange rates, cash or credit, Uber vs taxi, drinking water quality, can you flush the toilet paper, physical maps of your new destination.*
- *Establish a routine to stay grounded during your long-term travels.*
- *Do a final sweep through of belongings at all your accommodations before you head out.*

12

THE GREATEST GROWTH EXPERIENCE
OF A LIFETIME

HOME SCHOOLING WHILE ON THE ROAD

"Travel is not a reward for working. It's education for living." – Anthony Bourdain

---

One of the most overwhelming aspects about our long-term travel plans was thinking about homeschooling our 11-year-old daughter while vagabonding. Scott and I had come from a long line of public and private schools. Scott went to a private school from pre-K until graduation, and I followed the same track through the public school system.

When we were making the decision on where to launch Kayla's educational path, we examined both opportunities, but homeschooling never entered our minds as a possibility. We were working full-time and knew that neither of us had the capacity to educate our daughter ourselves, at home. Ultimately, Kayla attended our neighborhood elementary school from kindergarten all the way through fifth grade and thrived in that structured environment.

About five months out from our departure, I decided to dip my toes into the expansive and unknown world of homeschooling. I honestly had no idea where to begin, so I did the simplest thing I could think of and Googled "homeschooling." Much to my horror, about 1,000 different ads popped up trying to persuade me as to why their schooling method was the best for my child. I had no idea there was such a variety of options and programs from which to choose.

All my fears rushed into my gut and sent a crushing blow to my confidence. *Can we really do this? Will we have the ability to educate our daughter effectively for a whole year?* I envisioned her returning to public school for seventh grade totally clueless and set back from her classmates. Kayla added to my anxiety when she said, "Mom, you don't know as much as my teachers. How am I going to learn anything? I'll be behind all of the other kids when I return."

Following a week of internal sulking, I spurred up some investigative motivation and reached out to a few people who had been homeschooling their children for years. They were a huge assistance in providing a 10,000-foot view of home-schooling program options and gave me several resources to help narrow the search.

But after funneling through Unschooling, Charlotte Mason, Classical, Montessori and religious-based homeschooling options for hours on end, I was exhausted. Nothing seemed to be the perfect fit for Kayla's learning style and my precon-ceived ability to teach. Frustrated, I walked away from my search for a while and took some time to contemplate a format that would work best for *our* family under *our* unique conditions.

I did not want to be trapped in the confines of someone else's program when we had an incredible opportunity to learn so many things from the big, wide world we were about to explore. I desired flexibility with curriculum content and a timetable so we could flow through our journey without the constraints of a defined schedule.

I glanced over the sixth grade curriculum that had been given to me by my friend who was a junior high principal. I made a phone call to the guidance counselor at Kayla's proposed middle school to explain our situation. I wanted to be clear about the course requirements needed to enter seventh grade after Kayla had spent a year away from traditional school.

Imagine my surprise when she told me that, in Texas, all I had to do was make up a report card showing Kayla's grades for five core classes.

"Really?" I asked her in astonishment. "You mean, I don't

have to maintain records of all her activities, test scores, projects and paperwork?"

"Nope."

"No final or reentry exams to prove her knowledge base?"

"Nope."

Yahooey!

With this vital piece of information, a green light immediately turned on and creative juices began to flood my brain. I pulled my big girl panties on and declared that instead of selecting a formal homeschooling program, we were going to *develop our own curriculum* wrapped around exposure to real-world, international wisdom—a truly global education at its finest.

A huge wave of relief rushed through me and I developed a new-found self-assurance in my teaching abilities. "The best education is through real-life experience!" and "Parents are the ultimate teachers!" became my new mantras.

I read an excellent book, *The New Global Student* by Maya Frost, which further inspired my creativity and expanded my view about what education can look like in our connected, modern world. My excitement built with the prospect of endless learning opportunities not just for Kayla, but for my entire family during our travels. At the end of the day, isn't that the whole point of exploring foreign lands?

Kayla could spend countless hours in front of her computer screen solving word problems, or she could be living in an exotic country solving *real-world* problems. The latter sounded much more appealing to me. We received a little slack from our friends and family when we publicized our decision for this lax school agenda. It was to be expected and was solely based on their own personal fear and unfamiliarity with thinking outside the box.

As you know, it is challenging to catch up on math lessons if you have not mastered the previous sequence of information, because modules build on prior instruction. I had not done sixth grade math in more than 30 years. In the end, to assist all of us, we chose an online curriculum called IXL to keep Kayla on track for math. As for the rest of her teachings, we opened our hearts to universal guidance!

Reflecting back, the experience of being a teacher at Goyette Academy, as we lovingly liked to call it, was challenging, eye-opening, rewarding and incredible all at the same time. With

Principal Mr. Goyette's support, acting as teacher Mrs. Goyette, was one of the most mind-expanding growth opportunities of my life. Although, Kayla may have had a totally different perspective on the whole mom being her teacher thing.

Developing a stimulating and engaging curriculum for Kayla stretched my brain capacity to its limit as I created each lesson on-the-go throughout our venture. My focus was to weave the local history, culture, customs, geography, religion and topography of each place we traveled to into lessons that would appeal to Kayla's learning style, interests and hobbies. It sounded like a big undertaking but once I got rolling, I was amazed to find how easily I was able to incorporate those topics into her core classes.

Fortunately for us, back home in Texas, the sixth grade social studies curriculum was centered around world history. While kids in Kayla's class were studying the Panama Canal, we were in Panama City hanging over the balcony railing watching the ships come into the locks. And, while sixth graders were learning about Mayan culture, Kayla was visiting Lake Atitlan, in Guatemala, taking part in a cacao ceremony led by a native Mayan shaman.

We read *The Diary of Anne Frank* to begin a month-long study of World War II as we traveled through Eastern Europe. We ended this lesson in Poland with an emotional tour of the Auschwitz and Birkenau concentration camps to witness the devastating loss of life and hear personal stories of the suffering endured during this period in history.

We studied the life cycle of the Magellanic penguin in Patagonia and took a boat trip to an island off the coast of Southern Chile to observe the activity in their breeding colonies. While in Patagonia, we hiked to a glacier lake in Torres del Paine National Park and did a research project on the water cycle in this frigid land.

We read about Greek Mythology, tasted the "Nectar of the Gods" at a local honey farm and skied from the top of Mount Olympus in Cyprus. And what better way to learn Spanish than to live in Spanish-speaking countries for six months? Talk about a first-hand education. Yes!

One of the benefits of home schooling internationally is that there are no rules or red tape to prevent you from doing things that would never be permitted to do in the U.S.

For example, Kayla loves to cook so I looked all over Talca, Chile for some fun cooking classes for kids but couldn't find any. I sent a note to a local bakery and they invited Kayla to their shop to bake with them on a weekly basis for the entire seven weeks we lived in the small town. What an incredible way to enhance her skills in "La Cocina", learn the metric system *and* get a Spanish lesson all in one.

If I were to try to do the same thing in the States, Kayla would need to be licensed, trained and meet the minimum age requirements for working, which would have meant missing out on this exceptional opportunity.

Propelled by Kayla's interest in becoming a chef, we engaged in cooking classes all over the world. We learned the local cuisine in Thailand and Sri Lanka and got fabulous lessons on how to incorporate their exotic spices into flavorful dishes. We picked up cookbooks in Poland and Costa Rica to understand the ingredients for native recipes. We had a private cooking class at a vineyard in Argentina and learned the art of homemade brick-oven pizza. And, above all, who else should teach you how to bake macaron cookies but a pastry chef in Paris.

As you can see, I was not the only teacher employed by Goyette Academy. As we moved around the globe, we solicited hundreds of experts to educate Kayla (it was for all of us, really) about their passions and proficiencies in their industry. There were so many hands-on educational resources for our child to tap into, which provided impactful learning experiences to be remembered for a lifetime.

If you plan your travels wisely, you can afford to embark on once-in-a-lifetime, enlightening (and affordable) opportunities for you and your child. For instance, we did an online investigation into the differences between Asian and African elephants and then spent a full day bathing, walking and feeding a herd of Asian elephants at a sanctuary in the mountains of Thailand for around $100 per person, including meals and transportation. On another occasion, we hired a private tour guide in Cambodia for only $40 per day to examine the magnificent architecture, religious history and hidden gems of Angkor Wat, the largest religious complex in the world.

I relied on these incredible resources for interactive learning experiences for Kayla at the highest level throughout our entire trip. This took significant pressure off of me trying to fulfill the unrealistic role of acting as her sole education provider. Guided tours, museums, national parks, train rides through the country, and more were all excellent sources for a top-notch, unforgettable education. These first-hand experiences made her international scholastic adventure so much more enjoyable and memorable – for all of us.

Logistically, our school schedule looked very different than a traditional school day. We had to be flexible around transportation restrictions such as flights, trains and car rides. Kayla accomplished much of her reading and writing while en route to other destinations, and she took advantage of Wi-Fi access at airport lounges, hotels and Airbnbs to work on her IXL online math program. The rest of her school time was spent researching the native culture, history, religion and geography and coordinating hands-on experiences that aligned with her investigations. Exploring the world in this way was an education of a lifetime, not just for our daughter, but for our whole family.

If you ask Kayla what she thought about homeschooling while traveling, you will hear her reluctantly saying "It was OK." Desperately missing her friends and the comforts of home as any eleven-year-old would had a significant impact on her outlook of her experience. Yet, when questioned by friends and family about her favorite parts of the trip now, you can catch an inkling of achievement and pride bubbling up in her eyes as she witnesses the awestruck looks of her audience in reaction to her adventures.

By the time May rolled around and we had been homeschooling for eight months, I was ready for summer break and it appeared Kayla felt the same way. If she had been attending school in Texas, she still would have had one more month before summer vacation but as it stood, she had completed not only sixth grade, but all of seventh grade math too. She had read eight high-level books on an array of topics and developed endless creative writing projects. She had entered countless international art contests and could hold a basic conversation in Spanish. I would say all of that was quite the accomplishment.

Considering she was so far ahead in her studies, we both decided that Goyette Academy would be in permanent recess starting May 1. I printed out a Certificate of Completion and we held a graduation for Kayla in our hotel room. Of course, she was valedictorian of her class and voted "Most Likely to Succeed". She also got the Citizenship Award and honors for perfect attendance. I produced her report card of straight A's (which she had truly earned) and emailed it to her counselor as proof of her competencies.

I was relieved to have the responsibility of Kayla's home-school education behind me. Although, at the same time, I felt a little twinge in my heart knowing that our formal relationship of teacher-student was no more. I was surprised at how much I had enjoyed being an active participant in Kayla's education and I was even more astonished at my own abilities and creativity.

I must say, homeschooling expanded my belief in my teaching capabilities way beyond my limited initial view. It stretched me past my outer limits and provided the single largest growth opportunity of my life to date. I am forever grateful for the experience.

The night before starting seventh grade in public school, back at home, I could tell Kayla seemed nervous.

"What if I don't know as much as the other kids? What if I'm behind?" she expressed to me, all her fears coming to the surface.

I reminded her of the incredible real-life experiences she had attained while traveling and assured her that she was going to be way ahead of the other students in all subjects. However, I sensed she didn't believe me.

About a week into the school year, Kayla rushed home and greeted me with enthusiasm. She was overjoyed about having breezed through her assessment test in math and super excited about understanding all of the words in her Spanish class.

I just gave her a big smile, though secretly inside a huge "Yahooey!" arose from the depths of my soul. *Awesome job, Mom!* I thought and gave myself a figurative pat on the back.

We did it!

And you can do it too. All you need is a little bravery, and a willingness to broaden your mind and think outside the standard educational box.

Now, you may have to do a little research of your own about your local school curriculum requirements, as they differ from state-to-state. And you might want to take some time to contemplate the best school year and age for your children to travel based on their individual personalities, educational flexibility and willingness to depart from their friends for an extended period of time. But the legwork you do upfront will be well worth the mind-expanding experiences you will expose your family to while traveling. A global education for your kids is literally at your fingertips if you dare to dive in and take a chance. Now jump!

Key Things to Consider

- *Traveling provides boundless opportunities for learning.*
- *Choose a curriculum that supports your teaching style and your child's learning style.*
- *You do not have to be the sole provider of your child's homeschooling education. Therefore, get help when needed.*
- *Rely on the vast resources of the world as your main teaching tools to create real-world lessons and offset the focus of a strictly online education.*

13

FAKE IT TILL YOU MAKE IT

MISTAKES TO AVOID ALONG THE WAY

"The only real mistake is the one from which we learn nothing." – Henry Ford

---

We made so many huge mistakes during our travels. Therefore, one of my biggest intentions for writing this book was to assist future vagabonders in skirting around the same faux pas we stumbled into. And believe me, we grappled with a few doozies. So, here I present the gory details of our outrageous blunders!

Trapped on Gilligan's Island – Know Your Outermost Limits

Our first debacle happened early on in our trip. We were visiting Medellin, Colombia, where we spent four nights at an incredible Marriott hotel in the heart of Pablado, a very trendy part of town. The hotel had every amenity you could think of including a delicious all-inclusive buffet breakfast, access to the executive lounge for snacks, a complete gym and a beautiful room that opened out onto the pool with a gorgeous view of the city.

Needless to say, we were quite spoiled with this full-service luxury and enjoyed every minute of it. We were also very excited for the next leg of our trip to Nuqui, Colombia, a miniscule, village inhabited by indigenous communities on the Pacific gulf. Our plan was to stay with a friend of a friend who owned a "retreat" home in the middle of nowhere.

The place came highly recommended by our friend and Scott did his due diligence by speaking with the owner several times prior to our departure to get a sense of what the experience would entail. She described her property as an incredible facility that could potentially be our next yoga retreat destination. We jumped at the opportunity and fantasized about this lovely boutique resort where the jungle meets the ocean.

Our host family picked us up at the tiny single-strip airport and casually suggested that we get some groceries in town. Little did we know at the time that this would be the only opportunity to access supplies for our entire twelve-day stay. They took us to a 20-foot x 20-foot shop that offered a limited supply of beans, rice, eggs and a few other products. We looked into the small meat freezer and saw a frozen one-eyed chicken staring up at us, split in half from head to toe. With that, we decided to go vegetarian for the next two weeks of our stay. We grabbed a couple of avocados, a bag of rice and beans, some eggs and were off.

It was a 45-minute ride on a small motorboat to reach our hosts' home. On the way we saw incredible humpback whales breaching in the distance, August being their birthing season. As we approached the shore near the house, to our surprise our hosts suddenly shouted "OK, jump!"

We looked around for a boat dock but there was none to be found. To our bewilderment, we had to jump into the ocean where the water was waist-deep and carry all our belongings above our heads up to the shore. We unsuccessfully dodged the waves crashing on our backs, trying to prevent our computers and cell phones from getting drenched—our precious lifelines to work, school and our only connection to back home. I could not believe that all of this effort was required every time our host family wanted to bring supplies to their house!

Once on shore, we hiked up a small hill to our accommodations. The poor condition of the structure froze us in our tracks, and we stood there in disbelief. Our promised retreat-style lodging was in actuality a totally open-air house with no windows, no doors, no AC, no refrigeration, no electricity and no hot water. The outdoor kitchen had a two-burner propane stove, and the water was pumped in from a nearby waterfall. It landed in your cup, gritty and brown, and had to be boiled every time you wanted to have a drink. Essentially it was camping with a roof over our heads and a bed with a mosquito net—a far cry from the extravagant accommodations we had been promised.

Nonetheless, I loved it! I am a nature enthusiast at heart, so I immediately connected with the fresh air and the sound of the waves crashing just a few feet from our "house". I enjoyed waking up every morning, sitting quietly by myself and watching pods of dolphins swim by. I loved picking limes and hibiscus flowers off of the nearby trees to make tea. I got creative and found 101 ways to cook eggs, beans and rice, which were our only food supplies for our entire stay.

My "Amenity Man" and "City Girl" counterparts had very different feelings, however. They felt totally trapped, like they were stranded on Gilligan's Island. As the show's theme song captures, "No phone, no lights, no motor car, not a single luxury. Like Robinson Crusoe, it's primitive as can be," this is what we were experiencing. Scott and Kayla were miserable!

Although our stay was not truly on an island, the only way to access the "retreat" was by boat, and we were totally reliant on the owners for connection to civilization. Since there was no Wi-Fi and no cell phone service, we had no way of contacting anyone and no one knew our location in the world. I have to admit, it was a weird feeling being so totally disconnected.

The experience was a forced and total detox of technology, alcohol, dairy, gluten, sugar and caffeine. By the second day my travel buddies were losing their minds. Factor in that they were both severely covered from head to toe in bites and had nowhere to escape the heat, they were not happy campers. The same sound of the waves crashing near the hut that lulled me to sleep kept them wide-eyed and awake all night. By the second night, they were begging me to get out of there.

We talked to one of the owners about our dilemma, but she was not willing to refund our money. Since we could not afford to pay for another place to stay, we decided to suck it up and make the most of our time there.

Luckily, the owners had six cats, a baby bunny and a bird, so that kept Kayla entertained for several hours every day. We cooked all our meals together and were mindful not to waste one drop of food because we had access to so little. Scraps that normally would have been thrown away were carefully saved in a Tupperware container for the next meal. Water that was boiled for cooking was repurposed for tea at a later time. We went for walks on the beach, stacked rocks on the shore, read and played tons of games. There was no technology to distract us. We only had each other.

One day the owners took us on a boat ride to a neighboring town. We were planning on going to some thermal springs and have lunch at the only "restaurant" there (a small hut on the beach). Our host stopped by the shack and asked what meal they were preparing for the day. They said fish soup and fish. I knew Kayla wouldn't eat fish, so I asked if they had any other options. They inquired if she liked chicken and I said yes. "Great!" they said, "Come back in an hour and it will be ready." As we walked away, I heard the squawk from a nearby rooster. I turned around and to my horror saw him being dragged out back to his demise, only later to be served on a plate as Kayla's lunch.

In the end, we only made it eight out of the twelve days that we were planning to stay. By the last day, Kayla had ripped off all her skin from scratching so much and Scott had lost 14 pounds, as well as his mind, on the Gilligan's Island diet. They were desperate to go home.

Although my teammates had suffered significantly, I thought it was a wonderful experience for our family. With no diversions or distractions, we spent quality time with each other. I can't remember the last time we cooked all of our meals and ate every serving of food together. It gave us the opportunity to get creative and make up fun things to entertain each other.

We spent 90 percent of the day outside in nature, in the sun and in the rain, with our feet touching the earth. We talked about our dreams (specifically what foods we missed the most). We were so appreciative of every meal, no matter how simple. We turned each leftover morsel into something delicious. Most important, we were all so grateful to have the basics: food, water, shelter and each other. We realized how very little we needed to be happy.

The experience reminded me of how fortunate I am to have access to so many resources back home. It is crazy that we can order something on Amazon and have it arrive at our door in four hours. On the other hand, in the majority of the world, if something breaks a replacement may not be attainable for months, or ever. Realizing the extensive variety of products that are available to us also blew my mind. It is unbelievable that we can go into a store in Austin like Whole Foods and have 20 different choices of milk, whereas most other people in the world only have access to powdered milk or nothing at all.

After eight days, since there was to be no refund, we said, "screw it!" and caught the first flight out the next morning. As the cold air-conditioning on the airplane hit our faces, I heard a sigh of relief from my companions. We headed to the same Marriott where we had first begun. At next morning's breakfast buffet, the normal tune from my daughter of "there's nothing to eat Mom," was replaced with "this is the best piece of bread I have *ever* eaten!" Our appreciation level skyrocketed with every warm shower, clean pillow and cold drink.

This challenging event significantly expanded our levels of patience to better accept the little annoyances that we experienced later on during our months of travel. To this day, if the Wi-Fi goes down for a minute, the meal isn't exactly the way we like it, they are out of an item in the grocery store or the shower isn't quite hot enough, we reflect back on our deserted island adventure and say, "It's better than Nuqui!"

The moral of the story? Do your research. I am not saying that every part of your trip has to be flawlessly laid out, where you are 100 percent confident in your plans. In fact, part of the fun is stepping into the unknown and allowing your journey to unravel before you. However, if you expect to explore a region for a longer period of time, it might behoove you to invest a little extra elbow grease on investigating your destination before you commit. This point applies doubly if you are traveling with children.

It is important to be familiar with the maximum capacity each of your nomadic companions can withstand and fly just under those boundaries. The Goyettes quickly realized that two out of the three in our party were stretched well beyond their limits in the above scenario and it made for a tough experience all around.

One Night in Bangkok – Check the Expiration BEFORE You Leave

While traveling in Thailand for two months, our family decided to take a couple of quick excursions to discover some other Southeast Asian countries. Scott found a great buy where we could take a short flight to explore Vietnam, travel onto Cambodia and then back to Bangkok. He booked the flights and discovered some incredible accommodations in Hanoi and a cool resort in Siem Reap, just outside of the Angkor Wat temple complex.

We were good-to-go with our itinerary. I decided to look up the requirements to enter the countries to see if we needed to acquire a visa. And I am so relieved I did! There was a hefty visa requirement for Vietnam that needed to be completed before arrival and took several days to be approved. I began filling out the online form and entering our passport information. As I was completing Kayla's application, I glanced at a warning that popped up when I typed in her passport expiration: "Passport Must Not Expire Within 6 Months of Entering the Country".

Oh crap! Before we departed for our year-long trip, I had checked to make certain none of our passports would expire before we returned back to Austin. Unfortunately, I never confirmed that they would not expire six months prior to our travel dates while on this next leg of our trip. The expiration date was one month short for Kayla's documents and we planned on flying to Vietnam in just two weeks!

In a total panic, we scrambled down to the U.S. Embassy in Bangkok to see if there was any hope. After waiting an hour and a half in line, we finally made it to the counter and pleaded our case to the clerk. They said we could apply to renew Kayla's documents, but most likely it would not arrive in time for our travels to Vietnam. We enquired about expediting the process and we were told there was no such opportunity.

Desperate, we decided to take our chances and started the procedure. However, the process was not easy. First, we needed to get hold of Kayla's birth certificate from back home. Luckily, they accepted an electronic version, and my parents were able to email us a copy.

Then, we had to provide passport photos. Typically, this

would not be a big deal if you were in the U.S. You could hop on down to any pharmacy store and get them done in minutes. However, we were temporarily residing in the most chaotic city in the world where nothing was easy. Driving three miles in a tuk tuk could take an hour. Therefore, getting to the photo shop was a scary feat in and of itself!

In addition, for a minor, we needed to provide pictures of us as the parents, with the child, from birth to her current age, to prove we were not trying to kidnap her. It took a full day's work to gather up all the proof that Scott and I were Kayla's legitimate guardians.

We slogged our way back to the U.S Embassy with all our evidence. After Kayla received a thorough interrogation from the clerk to again confirm that she had come from my womb and belonged with us, we submitted the paperwork and hoped for the best.

Luckily, we had two more weeks of travel in Thailand before we were expected to take our flight to Vietnam. So, it was possible that we could get her renewed passport when we passed back through Bangkok on our way to the airport. Still, the chances were slim.

We chose to leave those worries behind us for the moment while we explored the mountain region of the north in and around Chang Mai. Our thoughts were temporarily occupied by the pristine scenery, auspicious temples and savory cuisine. Meanwhile, we had no idea where our application was on its long journey across the Pacific Ocean to the U.S. and back again.

When our two-week stay in Thailand was complete, we headed back to Bangkok. We had one day before our upcoming flight to make it to the embassy and see if we were destined for Vietnam. Our travel fate was in the hands of the U.S. government, which was not a good place to be.

We waited another hour in line and were finally called to the counter by the same clerk from our prior visit. Fingers crossed behind our backs and shit-eating grins on our faces, we held our breath while he checked to see if our documents had arrived. He appeared from the back office with a big manila envelope marked **KAYLA GOYETTE** in bold letters. A huge collective exhale signaled the pure relief and joy we felt on realizing our good fortune. Off to Vietnam we went!

You can travel the easy way or the hard way. My recommendation is to plan for ease. First and foremost, make certain ALL your documentation has plenty of wiggle room for the expiration date throughout your travel time. That includes your driver's license as well. We ran into the same challenge in Cyprus because Scott's driver's license expired during our travels. We found out the hard way that you cannot rent a vehicle with an expired driver's license. Let our mishaps be your lessons-learned and plan accordingly.

Halloween vs. Dias de Los Muertos – Research Cultural Customs and Traditions

We arrived in Guatemala late in the evening on October 30th, the day before Halloween. For Kayla's sake, I Googled to see if Guatemala City engaged in trick-or-treat practices on Halloween eve. I found out that, although not as popular a holiday as in the U.S., some of the kids in the city got dressed up in costume and went trick-or-treating in the malls. I was excited to be staying in a country that acknowledged the holiday and also celebrated Días de Los Muertos, the Day of the Dead, on November 1st. It was perfect timing to be able to commemorate both festivities and experience them first-hand.

We spent the next morning running around town searching for a zipper and some glue. Kayla is quite the makeup artist; our plan was for her to transform my face into a sugar skull, a decorative human skull representing the Mexican Day of the Dead, creeping out of a partially opened zipper. She worked all Halloween eve adhering the zipper to my skin and designing her masterpiece using watercolor pencils she had on hand. You learn to be very resourceful while on the road with access to limited supplies.

Her creation was a shocking success. I looked absolutely eerie and was thrilled that my costume fit the theme of the local celebration. Kayla put the finishing touches on hers and Scott's skeleton costumes and we prepared to head out to hit the streets of Guatemala City in search of a mall and some sugary delights. We were excited to see all the kids dressed up and experience how this foreign country honored such a coveted American holiday.

We stepped out from our hotel onto the sidewalk and looked around, expecting to be surrounded by ghouls and goblins. It was immediately apparent that we were the ONLY ones in the entire city in costume. Everyone glared at us like we had twelve heads as we made our way to our shopping destination through the crowded streets of people dressed in business attire. We were totally out of place and embarrassingly stuck out like sore thumbs.

We popped into a coffee shop to ask where the closest mall was located and decided to stay for a drink while waiting for our Uber ride. I sat next to an open window so I could people-watch and heard a little boy singing "Chiclet, Chiclet!" trying to sell gum. He stepped up to the window to make me the offer, took one look at my spooky face, screamed from the unexpected shock and ran away. I guess I really messed up on my read for how Guatemalans celebrate Halloween!

"All the kids are probably dressed up at the mall," I assured Kayla, as we hopped into our ride and scared the crap out of our driver. I held my breath as we walked into the shopping center, praying it would be filled with children enjoying all their goodies from the store merchants. Yet, sadly, we were the only ones to take this American holiday so seriously.

We strolled around the shopping mall and could not find a single vendor giving out candy. I was crushed more than anyone because I felt guilty that Kayla was missing out on all the fun back home. We ambled by a candy shop and the store owner took pity on us. She gave Kayla a beautiful box of colorful delicacies. With her prize in hand, we ducked into a theater to watch the Halloween-themed movie *Goosebumps* in Spanish. We finished the night in a restaurant eating Chinese food and got the evil eye from the waiter along with several other patrons. It ended up being a very different night than we expected—although the unexpected is half the fun when maneuvering around foreign lands.

After that debacle, we made sure to do plenty of investigation before engaging in any other indigenous traditions. Especially in countries like Japan, you do not want to insult the native people and humiliate yourself when fumbling through their local customs. Take it from my experience, do your research!

Did Someone Say Two for One? – Wear Your Passport on You at All Times

In addition to enabling you to enter and exit different countries, passports are used for a variety of reasons internationally. A valid passport is required to check into hotels, Airbnbs and other vacation rentals. It is also extremely useful when acquiring tickets for tourist attractions. You can often get a child discount if you can prove their age.

We learned this the hard way after waiting in an endless line in Cambodia to buy tickets for the Angkor Wat temple complex and found out we could have received a $20 reduced rate for Kayla if we had just had her passport with us. You will be surprised by how many occasions you need your passport when exploring the world, so keep it handy.

Blunder at the Barber Shop – Lost in Translation

At the launch of our trip, Scott, Kayla and I decided we wanted to grow out our hair for the entire duration of our year-long journey. The girls in the family already had long hair, so a few extra inches would not be a big deal for us. My husband, on the other hand, wore a more clean-cut look with his hair a little longer on the top and faded on the sides. He once sported a long, curly mullet with a tail in the 80s and thought this was the perfect opportunity to bring back his rock-and-roll style.

As the months rolled on, Scott's "fro" grew larger and larger. In our quarter of a century existence together, I had never seen his hair so fluffy. At first, he loved it because his lengthy locks represented the freedom he desired on our excursion. However, after a while, with his big hair growing at lightning speed, my OCD-inclined man started to lose his mind. By the time we were living in Talca, Chile, he could not take it anymore.

Since we were staying in Talca for seven weeks, Scott took the time to wander into a few barber shops to scope out the scene. My meticulous man wanted to make certain he chose the hairstylists who would cut his precious mane wisely. After visiting several salons, he noticed one hairdresser in particular who had a line out the door waiting for his services. "That's the one!" he reported to me. "He must be good if there are so many locals willing to wait."

The following day, he set off from our apartment to get his new "do". Kayla and I were working in the living room when I heard him return a couple of hours later. I looked up as he entered the room and saw a smile on his face. "What do you think?" he asked as he showed me the profile of his left side. It appeared the stylist had done a nice fade, which is the hardest part to get right on a man. "Looks great!" I said with relief, knowing how picky Scott was about his hair.

Within a second of completing my sentence, he flipped around to show me his right side. I gasped in horror! This whole half of his head was shaved almost bald up to the top of his crown and around the back of his neck with long locks left on the top. Business on the left, WTF on the right!

"What the hell happened?!" I asked in astonishment.

He shook his weary head in utter disappointment. He went on to tell me how this hair catastrophe had occurred. He was explaining to the hairstylist in Spanish that he wanted a subtle fade on the sides and to keep it longer on the top. He then adopted some hand gestures, using his index and middle fingers in a scissor-like motion relying on the universal sign for cut, to make his request clearer. Apparently, the barber translated his perfectly executed sign language as "Shave it to the top baby!"

Scott knew he was in trouble with the first passing of the electric razor and tried to stop the horrid action from continuing any further. But a quick peek in the mirror confirmed that it was too late. Somehow, Scott was able to convey his message more clearly about the second side. He walked out of the salon defeated...looking like half businessman, half punk rocker.

Of course, Scott's nerves could not leave his locks in such a mixed-up mess. He found a simple barber who evened out the sides and ended up with a hairdo more like a newly enlisted marine. Not quite the look he was going for, but it was better than the Dr. Jekyll and Mr. Hyde-version he had before.

A week later, I was hiking in the mountains of a local Chilean town with some newfound girlfriends. We took a break at a rest area and sat down at a picnic table to refuel with some snacks. As I was munching on a bag of granola, I looked over at the table next to us where a good-looking couple in their 20s were enjoying some rest as well. The man was handsome with a faded haircut on the side.

Suddenly, he turned around to look at something and to my surprise the other side of his head was shaved clean to the crown of his head and around the back with long strands of hair on the top. He had the same exact style as Scott! I slyly snapped a picture of his hairdo as proof to my husband that he had missed his chance to embrace a trendy Chilean hairstyle!

I can also attest to having a disastrous hair calamity of a different nature. Throughout our trip, Scott had become hair-dresser for Kayla and me, giving us small trims every few months to get rid of the split ends.

I am a brunette and typically like to maintain my grey roots to match my natural color. While traveling, it was challenging to find an identical color to my favorite brand of store-bought hair dye. I tried several different boxes the first six months of our trip and ended up with a rainbow of shades striped across my mane.

It was getting close to my birthday while we were in Bangkok and I wanted to look and feel my best for the occasion. I searched several stores for a suitable color dye, but could only find shades of black, which makes sense in a dark-haired nation. I figured I would have to bring in my 46th year looking like an old lady with grey roots. Scott knew my dilemma and suggested I splurge on getting my hair done at a local salon. After all, services were so cheap in Thailand, it couldn't cost that much.

As we made our way back to the hotel, we passed a beauty parlor located right across the street. Scott pushed me in the door and encouraged me to go enjoy some self-care time. The owner of the shop greeted me with a warm, friendly smile. She asked in broken English what I would like to get done. I enquired if she could match my natural color and just touch up my roots and she said, "No problem!"

I was so excited to treat myself to this luxury and have a few minutes of alone time. As the stylist mixed my color, we chatted about Thailand's culture and customs. It was so interesting to get the inside scoop on how my hairdresser and many Thai people felt about their current king and how the citizens were treated by the government.

An hour into the process, my hairstylist was still applying color. Several times, she commented about the tremendous thickness and length of my locks. She was not used to working with curly, coarse hair as most Thai people have fine, strait tresses. She sat me under the dryer for 20 minutes to activate the process and then took me to a sink to rinse out the dye.

"How is the color? Were you able to match the shade?" I asked. "It came out perfect!" she exclaimed with a smile. She plopped me in a salon chair with a towel wrapped around my head, my back facing the mirror. Just as she unwrapped the cloth and let my locks fall down my body, her receptionist walked around the corner into the room. Her wide-eyed look of shock as she stared at my head sent a clear message that this couldn't be good. *It can't be that bad*, I thought to myself hopefully.

Sounding pleased with herself, the owner spun me around to face the mirror and asked, "What do you think?"

The reaction to my reflection told it all. My natural brunette curls had somehow transformed into outrageously electric orange locks. I looked like a sad rendition of Ronald McDonald. I was appalled!

"This doesn't match at all!" I exclaimed. She tried to convince me that it was the perfect match, but I wasn't buying it. "No, no, no! You can't leave me this way!" I pleaded. She finally gave in and agreed to tone the color down a little. Before she did, I snapped a picture of my stellar new look and texted it to Scott with a statement: "I should have known better than to walk into a random salon in Bangkok!"

My confidence in her color mixing skills was not high, but after five hours in the chair, she finally pulled it off. I can only blame myself for making the decision to get my hair done in Asia, where the stylists' sole experience is working in shades of black. Lesson learned.

A White Trash Oversight – Don't Air Your Dirty Laundry

Scott did such an incredibly mindful job of planning out our accommodations throughout our travels. At least once a week, he would intentionally choose lodging that offered laundry facilities so we could freshen up our stinky clothes. Remember, we wore the same five outfits our entire trip. So, cleaning them was imperative if we didn't want to get kicked out of businesses or get funny looks because our stench was so wretched.

On the day in Colombia when we escaped from Gilligan's Island, we found ourselves landing up at one of the classiest hotels that we had stayed at during our trip. The Marriott Pablado in Medellin was refined in every way. From the top-notch executive lounge to the gourmet breakfast in the morning, the property was dripping in elegance in all the ways that mattered.

Unfortunately, the one thing it did not have was a laundry facility. And after living in dirt for eight days, we urgently needed to wash our clothes. Well, desperate times called for desperate measures. So, we walked to the nearest supermarket, bought a jug of laundry detergent, filled up our bathtub and began scrubbing the cooties out of our clothes.

My obsessive-compulsive man was in charge of the scouring and rinsing. I, on the other hand, was responsible for the wringing and drying. I looked around our room for a place to hang our wash, but I didn't want to get the beautiful wood floor soaked with our dripping wet laundry.

It was a warm, sunny day outside, so I opened up the back doors that led to our poolside deck. A couple of lounge chairs would do just fine as a laundry rack, I decided. There was no one at the pool that morning, so I spread the clothes out over several chairs—underwear, socks and bras included. Satisfied with my decision to let the rays of the sun do the drying, I went back inside.

Within 15 minutes of completing my job, there was a knock at the front door. Scott walked over and answered the call. The hotel manager appeared looking agitated. "Sir, you cannot hang your clothes on the pool lounges to dry. You will have to pick them up immediately or I will have to ask you to leave," he said in a stern voice.

I sat huddled in the back of the room listening in on the conversation. I squirmed when Scott turned towards me and shot me a piercing, mortified look, not aware of my laundry rack choice. He apologized to the manager, slammed the door and we both raced outside to collect our clothes, skivvies and all. I never felt so "white trash" in all of my life.

That being said, there were several times throughout our

journey where we found ourselves scrubbing in the tub. Word to the wise, make certain to choose a private area to hang your washed garments. Not smack dab in the middle of a chic hotel pool deck. Rub-a-dub-dub, three Beverly Hillbillies in a tub. C'est la vie!

Be assured, there is no doubt that you too will make your own mistakes while on your trip. There isn't any way to avoid these self-created challenges when you are enveloping yourself in a plethora of first-time experiences. Yet, these trials and tribulations were the core of our best travel tales. They made for the perfect muse to our funniest stories as we relayed our adventures to our friends and family.

People like to say, "What doesn't kill you makes you stronger." However, I prefer to express international faux pas in a different way. "What doesn't totally destroy you mentally, makes for a great pee-your-pants-in-fits-of-laughter story for tomorrow." So, remember, your stressful experiences are just good material for future, self-deprecating amusement!

∾

Key Things to Consider

- *If you can't laugh at yourself, who can you laugh at?*
- *Just roll with it!*
- *Fake it till you make it.*

14

HONEY, I'M HOME

REENTERING YOUR "REAL LIFE"

"There's no place like home." - Dorothy, *The Wizard of Oz*

Walking into our house after being gone for 12 months was so incredibly surreal. I sat down on the couch in the middle of my living room and just stayed there for a while looking around. I was in a daze. We were incredibly lucky to have had fabulous, mindful tenants who kept all of our belongings in excellent condition and precisely where we left them. It felt like someone had woken me up from a year-long dream and plopped me right back into my old life. Nothing seemed to have changed, except that … everything had changed.

At the start of our trip to incent Kayla to join our world travel escapade, Scott and I promised her a puppy immediately upon returning home. Just moments after touching down in Austin, we delivered on our promise. With the help of my parents, a wiggly, adorable puppy named Jimmy Kibble greeted Kayla as she stepped inside our home.

In a flash, we had transitioned from a family on a world adventure, with new experiences around every corner, to a family with a permanent home and a new puppy, back to doing our daily routine. To tell you the truth, it felt great to get grounded in stability for a while.

After living out of a suitcase for a year, I was ecstatic to finally unpack and put my things in a drawer. Sleeping in my own bed was a divine experience. Although, for the first few nights I would wake up, totally disoriented, and think that I was back in a Bangkok hotel.

I had missed everything about Austin. Being away for so long, the first experiences of enjoying the sweet smell of the summer air, eating P. Terry's Hamburgers and Texas BBQ and having reliable Wi-Fi made my heart sing. The day after returning home, I rushed out to my backyard and relished in spending the afternoon gardening barefoot and reconnecting with all my plants. Having access to my own plot of land where I could sink my fingers into the earth was one of the things that I missed the most while traveling. We all were so happy to be back in familiar territory surrounded by all our friends and family.

Before we left, Kayla had asked her best friend, Morgan, what gift she would like her to bring back from our travels. Morgan thoughtfully requested some tea from Japan, as she did not want Kayla to have to lug a big present around in her bag all year. My daughter took this request to a whole new level and gathered tea samples from every country we visited. She delivered on her promise and to Morgan's surprise, presented her with over 150 bags of tea! This bundle did not include the additional 150 bags of duplicate tea Kayla had collected for herself, so they could have a tea party together.

Although Scott and I came across a million gifts while traveling that we wanted to buy for our friends and family back home, we knew we could not carry them with us. Instead, we decided to take Kayla's lead and collect lightweight spices that represented countries around the world. The recipients of our presents were delighted with the opportunity to experience such a variety of international flavors.

The first few weeks back home were spent undoing everything we had done during our preparations to leave: changing our mailing address, transferring the utilities from our tenants back into our name and getting our cars up and running again were just some of the tasks we had to accomplish.

We reluctantly took a peek in our garage, where all our belongings had been stored in stacks of boxes that touched the ceiling, and quickly slammed the door again. Several more weeks went by before we mustered up the courage to tackle that space. Surprisingly, with all the purging we did prior to our travels, we now realized that if we had not needed it for a whole year then there was so much more we could give away.

I unloaded my clothes out of storage and it was like winning a wardrobe jackpot after wearing only the same five outfits for twelve months. Carrying all our belongings on our back brought a clear understanding that you need very little to be happy. Having access to all our "things" seemed excessive in comparison.

Traveling abroad heightens all your senses. Once you cease this forward momentum, you quickly realize that your elevated awareness has been running nonstop for 365 days straight. Your nervous system has constantly been in GO mode. There has to be a letdown at some point, and there was.

About a month after we had arrived home and become reacquainted with our newfound environment, it hit us like a ton of bricks. Our minds thought the world had stopped spinning. All the built-up energy required to accomplish every detail of this once-in-a-lifetime adventure came to a screeching halt and we underwent pure and extensive exhaustion. I believe this sensation is totally normal considering we were on the go for such a long period of time.

We hunkered down in our house for a while and took a massive life siesta. The great thing about our reprieve was that we finally had time to contemplate and assimilate all the incredible things we had done on our journey. It is challenging to fully appreciate the unbelievable events you experience on a daily basis when you are hopping from one dreamlike destination to another.

Imagine all the magnificent things you do on a week-long excursion and how tired you may feel from all the activity. Think about the time you spend after your vacation reminiscing about every bit of fun you encountered. Now multiply that by 52 consecutive weeks of endless adventure, and you got yourself a whole lot of experiences to absorb.

Luckily, we had the opportunity in our schedules to pause and savor those 365 days of adventure. Don't worry, we did recover from our bone-tiring fatigue in a relatively short amount of time and got right back to our lives! That is how it goes. You have to decompress to be able to enter back into your "old life".

We found ourselves jumping right back into our daily routine, almost like we had never left. I was very pleased that we arrived home in June, so we could have the summer to slowly ease back to our regular schedules before the rigidity of the school calendar started.

The first few months that we were home, we were invited to endless gatherings to reconnect with friends and family. Everyone was so interested to hear about our travels. *Which country was your most favorite in the world? What was the craziest food you tried? How friendly were the people? What was the most beautiful place you visited? Did you ever feel unsafe?* were questions that we answered over and over again.

Our repetitive responses began to meld into a beautifully displayed story of great animation and amusement. We weaved in the hilarious bloopers and blunders, awestruck moments and extensive challenges that we met as we invited our friends and family members along with us to relive our journey.

Instead of feeling taxed by answering these questions over and over, we became energized as we recalled the excitement of our escapade. Having the opportunity to express the exhilaration which we discovered on our trip to other people, not just one another, allowed us to finally soak up the details of our expedition. We were able to reminisce about our vagabonding in a totally different light than experiencing it directly. After all, once your trip is over, all you have left are the memories.

Throughout our journey, we used Facebook to post pictures of our adventures and keep family and friends up to date on our travels. I am so elated we did because after being home for more than two years, we are still getting popups of photo memories reminding us of where we were in the world on that day. These prompts are incredible keepsakes that take us back to a time and space when we were world explorers, never knowing what the next destination would bring.

You might think that after wandering from one exotic place to the other for a year, we would be bored and feel confined in our home. However, to tell you the truth, the grounded essence of staying put in a familiar place for a while was comforting to all of us. In fact, Kayla—to this day—has no desire to leave Texas, or Austin for that matter. She is extremely content with staying within a three-mile radius of home, visiting with her friends and playing with her puppy, Jimmy Kibble.

Admittedly, to satisfy our wanderlust, Scott and I had the opportunity to weave a little travel zing into the first six months of our return home. We tried to entice Kayla to join us, but she dug her heels in and it was apparent she was more than satisfied to enjoy the comforts of Grammy and Poppy's house while we set off to discover new territories. We embarked on a trek halfway around the world to teach a yoga retreat in fabulous Bali. This peaceful, Hindu island in Indonesia had always been on our bucket list and we felt so grateful to witness its beauty, culture, food and people first-hand.

It says that you can take the person out of the adventure, but you cannot take the adventure out of the person. Therefore, respecting Kayla's wishes to "never travel again" (at least for now), Scott and I have developed a fascinating plan for retirement that involves extensive discovery of uncharted lands and habitation in far-off nations to explore the wonders of the world.

If you want my advice (and if you don't, feel free to skip to the next chapter), it makes sense to consider re-entry into your "real life" as part of your travel escapade. Just like traveling in unfamiliar, new places, coming home may resemble a foreign land for a while. Discovering new restaurants and shops that opened up while you were away might be just the right amount of novelty you need to maintain interest in your hometown for a time.

Ultimately, when you start to sense that itch in your feet again, the travel bug longing for action, nothing can stop you from setting sail on another excursion to satiate the wanderlust that burns deep within your soul.

≈

Key Things to Consider

- *Upon returning home, make significant time for decompression and absorption of all your travel adventures.*
- *Consider re-entry into your "real life" as part of your travel journey.*
- *Use your time at home to get grounded and reenergize for your next travel escapade.*

15

THE VEIL HAS BEEN LIFTED

REFLECTIONS ON A LOOP AROUND THE WORLD

"We travel not to escape life, but for life not to escape us."
– Robyn Yong

In the months leading up to our great escapade, I noticed that I would wake up in the middle of the night with my jaw clenched so tightly I thought my teeth would break. I did not realize all of the stress that I was holding in my body and mind throughout the preparation process.

Yet, as soon as we launched our adventure, all of that pressure dissolved away, and I found myself relaxing into a peaceful slumber in the evenings. With every major transition that I have ever encountered, what amazes me most is the sense of calm and contentment that arises when I make it through to the other side.

There will undoubtedly be a build-up of emotional and physical energy before there is transformation. That energetic ascension provides the required momentum you need to create change. Furthermore, just like a caterpillar's transformation into a butterfly, once you crack open your chrysalis and take a peek out of your restricting container, you will feel a release like no other. You will have pushed through the veil of limiting beliefs and arrived in a world full of freedom and flow.

Had we given up when we felt the overwhelming press of fear about the unknown, we would have missed out on one of the most mystifying and fulfilling experiences of our lives. Do not allow the swelling of energetic force to freeze you in place on your journey towards evolution. Instead, embrace the temporary discomfort, as this is the exact power that is required to advance you on your path. The combination of energetic build-up and release to create change is the law of the universe.

That being said, my family of three quickly realized that transformation was going to be the underlying theme throughout our year-long excursion, whether we liked it or not. Our minds were sprung wide-open as we stumbled upon the most unusual people, animals, food and cultures that we had no idea existed on our planet. Our eyes could barely withstand the magnificent beauty we witnessed gazing at the exceptionally unique land-scapes we encountered in every corner of the world. Transformation is bound to happen when you free yourself from the confines of your small existence and open yourself up to the awesome splendor of our planet.

Exposure to endless first-time experiences is also an excellent way to crack open your limited thoughts and enlighten your perspective. We can safely say that the challenges of long-term world travel are what provided us with the most powerful occasions for personal growth. In all our lives, we had never been confronted with more problem-solving opportunities. On a daily basis, we were put to the test to see if we could "make it" in our foreign surroundings. One roadblock after the other appeared, we were summoned to conquer the challenge—and somehow, we always did!

We surprised ourselves with our immense capacity to master each situation as it unfolded before us. Sometimes not as grace-fully as we would have liked but we made it through, nonetheless.

Surviving togetherness 24/7 for a full 365 days was an accomplishment in itself for our trio. As you can imagine, tension builds pretty quick when you are living in small quarters and do not have a break from each other, even for one minute. I can still see the three of us sitting shoulder-to-shoulder on a queen-sized bed in a small hotel room, computers on our laps while we all attempted to work.

Many of our most memorable pictures were snapped just moments after a huge argument, faking happiness with gigantic smiles on our faces. One day, our threesome got into a big fight.

Kayla was furious at us for some reason and screamed "I'm out of here!" She stomped around our 250 square-foot hotel room in an angry circle then ultimately made her way back to her seat, plopping down in defeat. We all started laughing as we realized the comedy of the situation.

There was no place to retreat and blow off steam. We had to be present with each other and figure things out right then and there. And guess what? We are still here today to talk about it. If that isn't an opportunity for growth, I don't know what is.

The three of us coveted the little alone time that we were each able to attain while traveling. Planned solitude was a must; we wanted to walk away from our team journey alive and still loving one another. Whether we took a jog on the beach, went for a walk in the woods, doodled in another room or just sat by ourselves in a corner and stared at our hands, taking a break from each other would refresh our spirits and minimize potential future conflict.

Scott and I watched Kayla develop from a child into a young adult right before our eyes, as she maneuvered the hectic city streets of Bangkok with confidence or ordered her meal in Spanish at a Chilean restaurant. She made strong efforts to learn several words in each local language and her self-assurance skyrocketed with her newfound ability to communicate with people from all over the globe.

In addition to having once-in-a-lifetime, breathtaking experiences, our trip unexpectedly opened Scott's and my eyes to endless possibilities for retirement. This unforeseen gift allowed us to visualize ourselves living like royalty during our retirement in places such as Thailand or Sri Lanka, where our savings could stretch out for years. We could picture lavishing ourselves with daily massages for $10.00 a treatment and dining on local cuisine overlooking the crystal blue waters of the Andaman Sea as we feasted for just $5.00. The prospect of living large in retirement sparked a new curiosity within and ignited an extremely hopeful outcome for our future. We were so grateful to have been exposed to these options early on in life to assist us in manifesting our retirement dreams.

Conversely, if you think world travel will provide the opportunity to run away from your troubles, you are severely wrong. The Goyettes rapidly understood that the difficulties we experienced within our relationships and within ourselves showed up in full force and followed us around the globe. We struggled many times with our individual weaknesses. Ultimately, we had to dig deep and address our shortcomings in an unconventional environment, without the extensive support system we had developed back home. We were left to rely on our internal strength and the bond between the three of us to help our clan thrive throughout our epic journey.

Long-term world travel has been THE most challenging and rewarding experience of our lives thus far. Each one of us stretched our capacity to the limit in every way imaginable. Our growth was immeasurable and the skills we learned while on the road will now be applied throughout our lives. Our expansive expedition changed our makeup at the cellular level. We will forever be grateful to the heart-warming people, interesting places, diverse cultures and remarkable scenery that molded our extraordinary adventure.

Key Things to Consider

- *Transformation is inevitable when you step outside your limits.*
- *Your problems will follow you, even if you are halfway around the world.*
- *World travel opens your mind to endless possibilities.*

Visit www.justplanecrazytravel.com for all the travel resources you need to plan your own adventure and follow our journey on Instagram at #goyetteworldadventure.

EPILOGUE: THE GREAT PAUSE

THOUGHTS ON A GLOBAL PANDEMIC

"Don't worry about the world coming to an end today. It's already tomorrow in Australia." – Charles Schulz

---

My family completed our year-long voyage around the world in June 2019. Unbeknownst to us, the pandemic would hit about six months after our arrival home. Boy, was our travel planning unintentionally timed perfectly!

As the news of COVID cases started being reported in China during the winter of 2019 with rapid spread to other Asian countries, Facebook Photo Memories popped up, reminding us where we had been in the world exactly one year prior. Pictures of our visit to Thailand, Vietnam and Cambodia prompted a huge amount of relief that we had dodged a bullet by not being stuck overseas in the middle of all the pandemic chaos.

Several times throughout the frenzied year of 2020, friends and family members would comment about the good fortune of our travel timing. Many asked us, with sincere concern, "What would your trip have looked like if you were still traveling during COVID times?" Scott and I had plenty of time during quarantine to contemplate the answer to that question.

Yes, our excursion would have looked very different with all the travel restrictions and facility closures. We may have had to hunker down in a hotel room or an Airbnb for a time until we figured out a path to safer ground. Logically, this epidemic is real-world stuff and could have happened during any moment of our trip but isn't the whole point of exploring the globe to be exposed to genuine, real-world experiences? You can't find a more authentic experience than the world being forced to a screeching halt!

Your creativity, endurance and resilience will never be more challenged than under extreme conditions. We have all felt the stress of the great unknown throughout these unique times. Yet, when put to the test, we have seen people, businesses and societies reconstruct the fabric of their beings to address "The New Normal" in miraculous ways.

We witnessed imagination and visualization flowing forth at lightning speed to attend to the immediate needs of humanity. Notwithstanding the pure shock we absorbed in the early stages of the pandemic, humankind demonstrated their powerful spirit by manifesting and delivering on a new way of doing things. Inspiration gushed with every trial and tribulation as the human race confronted and conquered our worst fears, one by one. Sounds like the perfect training for making your world travel dreams a reality!

Living together on the road in close quarters 24/7 for 365 days, separated from friends and family, prepared us for the same challenges we faced during quarantine. Although, being confined to our own home also felt like a great opportunity to slow down and get grounded for a while.

Yes, the constrained and isolating conditions brought back a little travel PTSD for Kayla. However, just like the rest of the world, the forced togetherness inspired our creative juices to develop innovative twists on art ventures, culinary masterpieces, home projects and new streams of income. In addition, it made time for abundant self-examination and reflection. Viewing these challenges as opportunities to expand our personal development allowed us to evolve, no matter what the condition of the planet.

You do not need to travel far to expose yourself to novel discoveries and reprogram your brain to live outside your limited beliefs. Try sampling some exotic international flavors by ordering takeout from a local ethnic restaurant. Engage in conversation with someone who doesn't look like you to gain a better understanding of their views. Read a book about a foreign culture to comprehend the beauty in all beings. That, my friend, is the definition of growth!

Whether you feel more at ease investigating the boundaries of your own city or you are excited to hop in an RV and explore the country roads of your beautiful land, adventure awaits you. You just have to say YES!

On the other hand, if you are ready to dive straight into the Big Kahuna and take a leap towards your dreams of world travel, then you might be...Just Plane Crazy!

GET'R DONE!

Packing List
- ☐ Luggage, backpack, day bag
- ☐ Purse, wallet
- ☐ Computer
- ☐ Cell phone, earbuds, paperclip
- ☐ Chargers
- ☐ Camera
- ☐ Outlet adapters
- ☐ First aid kit
- ☐ Medications, supplements
- ☐ Toiletries
- ☐ Shoes, flip flops, sneakers
- ☐ Weather-specific clothing
- ☐ Flashlight
- ☐ Games, art supplies
- ☐ Journal, pen, pencil

ID Documentation, etc.
- ☐ Credit cards ☐ Bank card
- ☐ Passport ☐ Driver's license ☐ Passport photos

Preparation List
- ☐ Vaccinations
- ☐ Credit card travel alert
- ☐ Credit card fraud alert
- ☐ STEP Smart Traveler Notification Registration
- ☐ International cell phone plan
- ☐ Worldwide medical coverage
- ☐ Online banking
- ☐ Download music playlist
- ☐ Global Entry / TSA Pre-check
- ☐ Find support back home to pay bills etc.

Install Essential Travel Apps
- ☐ WhatsApp ☐ Waze ☐ Google Translate
- ☐ Insight Timer Meditation App

MAKING IT HAPPEN
EASY RESOURCE GUIDE

Funding Your Big Plan

- www.sabbatical.com - A home rental resource strictly for Higher Education personnel only.
- www.airbnb.com - Connects travelers with a wide range of accommodations.
- www.vrbo.com - A place to find vacation rentals.
- www.homeexchange.com - A website that connects two parties who agree to swap each other's homestays for a set period of time.
- fitnessprotravel.com - Offers affordable vacations in exchange for teaching fitness classes or offering wellness services.

An Adventure of a Lifetime with Zero Debt

Credit Cards

These are the highest-point loyalty credit card programs at the time of publishing this book. Offers change on a daily basis, so go to www.justplancecrazytravel.com for up-to-date tips on which travel credit card to choose:

- Chase United Club Mileage Plus Credit Card

- Chase Marriott Bonvoy Credit Card
- Chase Sapphire Reserve

Airline Loyalty Programs

- United Airlines Mileage Plus
- American Airlines AAdvantage
- Delta Skymiles

Online Booking Agents

- www.booking.com
- www.orbitz.com
- www.expedia.com
- www.travelocity.com

Need help discovering travel deals? Check out www. justplanecrazytravel.com for all the travel resources you desire.

What to Pack

- ☐ Packing squares
- ☐ Travelpro luggage
- ☐ High Sierra backpacks
- ☐ Bagallini purse
- ☐ Universal travel outlet adapter

Imperative Things To-Do Before You Leave

- ☐ Equifax (800) 525-6285 www.equifax.com
- ☐ STEP Smart Traveler Notifications www.step.state.gov
- ☐ Expat Global Medical
- ☐ Global Entry
- ☐ TSA Pre-Check

Homeschooling on the Road

- *The New Global Student* by Maya Frost
- www.ixl.com

Accommodations on Our Route

Costa Rica

- Anamaya Resort, Montezuma www.anamaya.com
- Dreams Las Mareas Resort, Guanacaste www. dreamsresorts.com

Colombia

- Marriott Hotel, Poblado Medellin

Chile

- Marriott Bonvoy Hotel, Santiago

Guatemala

- Villa Sumaya, Lake Atitlan www.villasumaya.com

Thailand

- Millennium Hilton Hotel, Bangkok
- Hilton Arcadia Resort and Spa, Phuket

Cambodia

- Royal Angkor Resort, Siem Reap www. royalangkorresort.com

Sri Lanka

- Marriott Hotel, Weligama Bay

Romania

- Hilton Hotel, Sibui

Poland

- Marriott Resort and Spa, Sopot

Spain

- Double Tree Hotel La Torre, Murcia

Things to Keep You Sane During Your Travels

Meditations

- Insight Timer Meditation App by Meditation Mutha
- *What Can I Become:* https://insig.ht/8mGgFTC9b
- *Healing Your Ancestral Lineage:* https://insig.ht/3V4YRHb9gb

Yoga Videos

- Yoga with Meditation Mutha YouTube Channel: https://youtube.com/channel/UC2IRjqNnjLNm0HH-NNPG_9Q

Spotify Playlists

- Playlists by Kimmy G

ACKNOWLEDGEMENTS

My editor Tatiana – for making the pages of this book come to life with your incredible wisdom. Thank you for being so patient with my third-grade grammar skills.

My book designer Paul – for your immense creative talents that manifested my vision into a reality.

My friends and fellow authors Mitzi and Patricia – for so graciously beta-testing this book and providing your honest feedback. I am so thankful for your guidance.

My friends Nuala, Beth, Lisa, Erika and many more – for being my sounding-board so I wouldn't rip my hair out during our travels. Thank you for helping me see the funny side of things.

My friend Laura – for your incredible support during the first draft of this book, and always. Your wisdom pushed me to step up my writing game and turned on my creativity.

My family: Gregg, Nancy, Jaxon, Grey, Susan, Paul, Jessica, Billy, Paul Michael, Deb and many more – for cheering us on throughout our adventure and beyond.

My best friend Alisa – for your consistent love and encouragement throughout this journey of life. Thank you for all your time and attention during the first draft edits. Our late-night emergency phone calls during the trip prevented me from losing my mind and kept me grounded. You are my rock.

My parents Ellen and Max – for allowing me to discover, dare and dream. My confidence and passion for life comes from your parenting. Thank you for all of the support you provided during our trip and that you provide always. My gratitude to you is boundless.

My daughter Kayla – for providing the single largest growth opportunity of my life. Being your mother has awakened me to what pure love feels like and I am so thankful to get to experience this incredible bond with you. Your witty humor and immense creativity inspire me daily.

My husband Scott – for helping me live outside my limits, for the laughs, for the adventure, for everything. I love you.

And to the countless people we met along the way who kept us safe, nourished our minds and bodies, filled our hearts with warmth and made our travel experience so incredibly expansive, I am forever grateful.

ABOUT THE AUTHOR

Kim Goyette is a yoga teacher, wellness coach, 70's girl, mother and lover of life. She enjoys all things nature, family, community, health, dance, rhythm, flow and freedom. As the owner of Meditation Mutha, her yoga and wellness business, Kim's passion is creating meaningful retreat experiences where people have the opportunity to connect with themselves and others, expand their limiting beliefs and thrive beyond their greatest imagination. Her wellness programs take participants on a journey to achieve their wildest life visions.

Kim and her husband also own Just Plane Crazy Travel, where they assist people every step of the way to live their world travel dreams. Kim resides in Austin, Texas with Scott, her hilarious husband of more than two decades, and her witty daughter, Kayla.

Find her on Facebook and Instagram @justplanecrazytravel and @meditationmutha and take one of her yoga classes on her Yoga with Meditation Mutha Youtube Channel. Visit www.meditationmutha.com to learn more about yoga retreats Kim is holding around the world and check out www.justplanecrazytravel.com for an abundance of vital travel resources.

instagram.com/justplanecrazytravel

facebook.com/justplanecrazytravel

TRAVEL NOTES

Made in the USA
Monee, IL
16 July 2021

73024643R00090